STARS

STARS

THE ART OF MAKING STELLAR GIFTS
AND RADIANT CRAFTS

KATY BROWN

PHOTOGRAPHY BY DEBBIE PATTERSON

SIMON & SCHUSTER

NEW YORK · LONDON · TORONTO · SYDNEY · TOKYO · SINGAPORE

For my two brightest stars, Hugo and Grace

SIMON & SCHUSTER

Simon & Schuster Building, Rockefeller Center

1230 Avenue of the Americas, New York, New York 10020

Copyright © 1993 Conran Octopus Limited

Text copyright © 1993 Katy Brown

Photographs copyright © 1993 Debbie Patterson

Photography on pages 56 and 106 by Henry Bourne

First published in 1993 by Conran Octopus Limited, 37 Shelton Street, London WC2H 9HN

Designed by Georgina Rhodes. Typesetting by Ian Muggeridge, London

Printed in China

10 9 8 7 6 5 4 3 2 1

Library of Congress Cataloging in Publication Data

Brown, Katy.
    Stars: the art of making stellar gifts and radiant crafts / by Katy Brown;
photograpy by Debbie Patterson.
        p. cm.
    Includes bibliographical references and index.
    ISBN 0-671-88436-0 : $23.00
    1. Handicraft. 2. Stars in art. I. Title
TT157.B785 1993
745.5--dc20   93-23144
                                                                  CIP

CONTENTS

. . . WHEN HE SHALL DIE,

TAKE HIM AND CUT HIM OUT IN LITTLE STARS,

AND HE WILL MAKE THE FACE OF HEAVEN SO FINE

THAT ALL THE WORLD WILL BE IN LOVE WITH NIGHT . . .

Romeo and Juliet, III, ii, 21-24

INTRODUCTION

Like other great writers before and after him, William Shakespeare used the stars to aggrandize and immortalize his heroes and heroines. In literature, art and religion throughout the world, stars have been similarly endowed with special metaphysical and mystical powers, yet they are usually depicted in a simplified visual form. From the four-rayed star which symbolized the sun god in ancient civilizations to the multi-rayed, elongated star of medieval religious iconography, this potent image has been stylized and regularized, making it perfect for ornamentation.

The physical reality of stars is so nearly beyond human conception that this simplification is hardly surprising. Those of us who are only vaguely versed in the complexities of astronomy find it difficult enough to imagine the Sun, our nearest star, for what it truly is: a vast self-luminous object that shines by radiation derived from internal energy sources, with a mass 300,000 times that of the Earth, and at least 93,000,000 miles away from it. When we discover that the nearest star to the Sun, Proxima Centauri, is about 4.3 light years further away, and that the most distant stars are in galaxies billions of light years away, yet still identifiable through telescopes, then the boundaries of our imaginations become distinctly tangible.

Human attempts to map the stars go back thousands of years, but lack of complete knowledge certainly hasn't prevented stars having a pervasive effect on many aspects of our lives. Before nautical maps were drawn up, both the Sun and stars were essential to ocean navigators, and their guiding role is mentioned in sources as ancient as Homer, Herodotus, the Bible and the Norse sagas. Armed with basic information about the movements of the heavens, the Phoenicians routinely imported tin from Cornwall by sea, early Polynesians crossed to Hawaii, and many shiploads of Vikings settled in Greenland.

Quite apart from this practical influence, some people attribute a more mystical power to the stars. According to astrology, the position of the stars at the time of birth pre-determines actions, passions and fate. Thanking your lucky stars and being star-crossed lovers are ideas springing from deep-seated beliefs.

In most religions, stars symbolize the presence of a divinity, the eternal, and hope shining in darkness. Queens of Heaven in both ancient and contemporary religions are crowned with stars, two of the best known being the Egyptian goddess Isis and the Christian Virgin Mary. Christianity has imposed stars on many of its visual interpretations of the saints – Bruno, Dominic and Nicholas among them – but its most powerful and significant use of the star as an image leading man to God is the Christmas star of Bethlehem which guided the Three Kings to the stable.

Judaism's Star of David, or in Hebrew, the 'Mogun David', meaning shield or protector, appears on the flag of the State of Israel, and most poignantly on the yellow badge issued by Nazis to Jewish prisoners of war. In response, the Star of David has been invested with the symbolism of heroism and martyrdom.

In the history of art and design, the star is typical of how geometric form has been derived from a natural source. When the earliest cave people translated the twinkling lights of the sky into multi-pointed shapes in yellow earth colors, they set the template of a star forever. It has become a universally recognized symbol and a favorite form in decoration; one which will never date and never go out of fashion.

Throughout this book there are stars for celebration, for decoration, and to delight everyone from babies upwards. Some ideas are inspirational, but most can be recreated at home. All of them have been designed and made by talented contemporary crafts-people, yet they are within the grasp of anyone who can follow the clear instructions. Read on and reach for the stars.

TWINKLE, TWINKLE, LITTLE STAR

It is the outer space mystery of
stars which so appeals to children.
They are easy to draw and
miraculous to look at in the dark.
With no evil associations, no
fear or threat, they have become
indispensable in decorating
children's bedrooms and
playrooms, and they feature
prominently in lullabies, rhymes,
and fairy-tales.
Use them to charm babies with a
simple mobile, to adorn
bedroom walls, and to print on
bed linen: in this chapter
we'll show you how.

COSMIC WALL FRIEZE

Transport children to a place way above their own little world by printing a fantasy wall frieze on a bedroom wall. Colorwash a wide strip at child height to use as a rough framework, then cut oversized rubber stamps to your own designs. Use block-printing inks for the best effect, and paint the finished frieze with flat varnish to seal and make it washable.

MATERIALS
Paper
Black felt-tip pen
Paper-cutting scissors
Glue
Dense rubber ¼inch/5mm thick
Metal-handled scalpel and blades
Dense foam rubber ¼inch/5mm thick
Rubber solution (as used in bicycle repair kits)
Blocks of medium-density fiberboard
(MDF) ½inch/1cm thick
Water-based block-printing inks
Saucers for mixing ink
Piece of mirror, glass, or large glazed tile
Linocut roller
Clear flat varnish

WORKING WITH RUBBER
When looking for rubber, use a scalpel for testing its hardness and density. It should be something like the rubber used for car tires, and should carve like hard cheese.

Above *Cut into the surface of the rubber stamps at an angle of 45 degrees to ensure sharp, clean lines.*

Right *Load the ink onto the stamp from a clean piece of glass or a tile, then practise printing on paper painted with emulsion before embarking on the wall.*

Practice cutting into the rubber before embarking on a stamp. Cut down into the rubber at a 45-degree angle away from the surface that will eventually print on the wall. If carving out a line on the design, cut down one way, then cut down again at 45 degrees to meet it, making a triangular carving in section.

CUTTING THE STAMPS
Draw your designs on paper. Keep them simple and appealing to children: here there are fantasy stars, moons with faces, simplified planets, and rockets, each of which covers a space of 4-6sq in/10-15 cm². They will print as mirror images of the drawings, so bear this in mind if they are to face a particular way. Using a black felt-tip pen, fill in all the parts that are to be printed in color. This helps to see the design as a print rather than a drawing and gives a clearer idea of where to make the cuts. Cut around the drawings, leaving an edge of at least ½in/1cm.

Spread a thin layer of glue on the back of the paper and stick firmly to a piece of rubber approximately 1in/2.5cm larger than the drawing.

Now start to cut the stamp. Score the outlines and shapes of the drawing through the paper onto the rubber. Peel off the paper guide and rub off any glue left on the

rubber. Now make the first cuts about ⅛in/2mm down into the rubber, at an angle of 45 degrees. Make the second cuts at an opposite 45 degree angle, to meet the first, and remove the strips of rubber. The outlines will show well now, but any surface of the rubber which is not to be part of the printing surface will still have to be removed. The blade will need to be held at a flatter angle to do this. It is easier to make rows of cuts until it is all cleared. Change the scalpel blades regularly, as they will blunt very quickly.

Trim away any unwanted edges and spend time cutting out straggly bits which will interfere with the clarity of the print.

It is essential to put foam rubber between your stamp and the MDF block because it allows for any irregularities on the wall surface. Cut out the foam rubber to the same size and outline as the finished stamp and, using the rubber solution, stick them together. Follow the instructions on the tube carefully. Using the same solution, glue the stamp to the MDF block. MDF can either be attached to the foam and the rubber in a square-shaped block or, preferably, can be cut to the same shape of your stamp with a bandsaw. Used in a square block, it will be more difficult to see the exact positioning of the print on the wall. Avoid the temptation to use ordinary lumber for backing the stamp; MDF is completely flat, strong, split-proof, and smooth to hold, which is important as it will act as the "handle"   for the stamp.

PRINTING THE FRIEZE

Plan the arrangement of designs on the wall and mark them in faint pencil. Decide on the colors and mix them to the desired shade in saucers. Mix plenty of each color ink. If it runs out and more has to be mixed, it may not be quite the same color. Experiment with how much ink is needed on the stamp: too much on the roller will smudge, too little will make a patchy print. Practice on lining paper coated with latex paint. Make sure the wall and the glass, mirror, or tile are clean and dust-free before starting to print.

Measure some ink onto the glass, and using the linocut roller, load the stamp carefully with ink. Press the stamp against the wall in the desired position. It may well

stick there, which will give you a chance to move your hands around making sure every part of the stamp's surface has come into contact with the wall. Do not let the stamp itself move, or there will be a shadowy outline around the design. The ink stays wet for a surprisingly long time, so there is no need to rush.

Carefully remove the stamp and let each print dry before you apply another one close by, to avoid smudges. When the whole frieze is completed and thoroughly dry, seal with a coat of flat varnish.

Below Don't feel hemmed in by the colorwashed strip – just use it as a guide. The frieze looks more fun if some stamps are shooting off into space.

ASTRAL MOBILE

A mobile is usually a baby's first toy. Bright colors, faces, and a gentle ever-changing movement are the perfect visual stimuli for encouraging a baby to focus. Three to nine weeks old is the optimum age to introduce a mobile, before babies try to reach out or to grasp, and just as they are beginning to recognize and to track objects.

In the 1930s, the American artist Alexander Calder had an exhibition in Paris of his abstract sculptures with moving parts, for which Marcel Duchamp coined the word "mobile", as opposed to his stationary abstract sculptures, which were called "stabiles." Calder tended to use motors to drive his mobiles: spheres or flat metal shapes moved up, down and round wires and rods at different speeds.

Heavy paper is the best material from which to make simple mobiles, because it sways in the slightest air movement, yet it has enough body to balance, to hold its folds and creases, but not to crumple. As long as the lengths of wire, tubing, and thread and the weight of paper given for this mobile are followed accurately, the balance will be right and will return to correct suspension when there is no breeze.

Right *The gentle, continuous movement of a mobile is mesmerizing and soothing for even the youngest baby.*

MATERIALS

24½in/62cm metal or plastic-coated wire

(½in/2mm diameter)

Strong black button thread or crochet cotton

10in/25cm metal or plastic tubing

Brightly colored construction paper

(in at least 3 colors)

Glue

Exacto knife

Steel ruler

Scissors

Pencil

Tracing paper

Compass or strong needle

Using the templates on pages 116-117, trace the outlines, dotted foldlines, faces and hanging holes for the sun, moon, and six stars on tracing paper. Transfer the tracings to the colored papers by pricking through the pencil lines with a pin. Make sure that each of the three large shapes has a small star in a contrasting color to hang above it.

Score the colored paper to a depth of about one-third of its thickness along the dotted foldlines. Curves can be drawn on in pencil first and then scored, either working freehand or by using plate or dish rims as a guide.

Cut out the outline shapes with scissors or an exacto knife and ruler. Crease and fold the paper along the scored lines, using both hands and folding the paper away from the cut side. Carefully pierce a hole for hanging in each piece using a thick needle or the point of a compass.

Cut the wire into two pieces measuring 16in/40cm and 8½in/22cm respectively. Follow the diagram (Figure 2) showing the positions of the wires and the lengths of thread. The length of thread from the sun to the wire is 5in/13cm; from the moon to the wire, 5in/13cm; from the star to the wire, 4in/10cm and from the top wire to the lower wire, 5in/13cm. The thread from which the mobile hangs can be of any length.

Cut the thread twice as long as the finished length, then following the knot diagram (Figure 1), double up the end and tie the thread in a knot as shown, forming a loop approximately 1¼in/3cm long. Attach the correct lengths of thread to the sun, moon, and star by threading the loop through the pierced hole and passing the knot through the loop. Cut the tubing into five lengths, each measuring 2in/5cm. Thread on a tube to conceal each knot, and then thread the relevant star above it.

Measuring the correct length of thread, attach the moon and star to either end of the shorter wire. Wrap the thread around the wire two or three times, knot it, and anchor it with a spot of glue ¾in/2cm from the end.

1 A simple sliding knot allows the two horizontal wires to be adjusted to give perfect balance. The paper shapes are attached to the thread using the same knot and loop method.

Trim off the tail end of the thread. Attach the sun ¾ in/2cm from the end of the long wire in the same way.

Loop a thread around the star/moon wire as illustrated in Figure 1 and secure it by passing the knot through the loop. Balance by sliding the wire through the loop until it hangs horizontally. Anchor it in place with a spot of glue. Thread on the tube and the small star, and attach to the top wire ¾ in/2cm from the end. Glue in place. Finally, loop the long thread from which the mobile will hang onto the top wire. Secure, balance, and finish off as before.

2 Plan and measurements for construction of mobile.

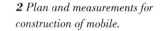

16 in

5 in

5 in

SUN

8 ½ in

5 in

4 in

MOON

STAR

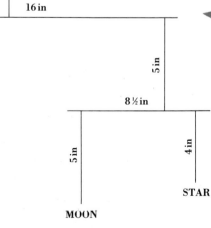

STARS AND STRIPES

Children's bed linen is often either mass-produced in manmade fabrics with garish designs, or rather preciously printed with bunnies and bows, and prohibitively expensive. To screenprint it yourself will guarantee the quality of the base fabric, allow for bold designs in good colors and make it truly original, as each printer will make a slightly different version.

This stars and stripes design is based loosely on the flag: uniform-sized blue stars on red striped ticking. The stars on the pillowcase are scaled down, but they could easily be varying sizes and be sprinkled rather than regimented. Stars look best superimposed on another geometric pattern, or else on a plain background, and of course any colour scheme can be chosen.

Screenprinting is an extension of stencil printing. Throughout history, people have duplicated images by piercing patterns out of leaves, paper, and fabrics and dabbing colors or dyes through the holes. The difference with screenprinting is that the stencil is supported by a frame holding tightly-stretched material, which results in more even and cleaner ink deposit. Using this technique, ink is forced through the open areas of the stencil and then through the weave of the material using a tool with a wooden handle and a flexible rubber blade called a squeegee.

An absolute prerequisite for successful screenprinting on fabric is to choose the right mesh for the job. A woven fabric such as cotton organdy will give the best result. Then it is important to have it properly stretched onto the frame, a process which is routinely and professionally done by screenprinting suppliers.

Dyes can be mixed according to the colors you want, and using a good binder with the dye makes it fast for washing, drycleaning, light, and general wear and tear. As a guide, 1¾ pints/1 liter of binder will cover up to 30sq ft/2.8m² of print area, and 1½oz/50g of dye color is enough for 1¾ -8¾ pints/1-5 liters of binder.

Cotton is an ideal fabric for printing on to, although most fabrics are suitable. Always test a small section before the whole batch is printed to make sure there is no special treatment on the fabric which might prevent even printing or color fastness.

Screens should be cleaned immediately and thoroughly after use using water and detergent. If the screen is stored with binder in the mesh, it will be permanently blocked and will be unusable.

Right *Widths of fabric should be screenprinted before being made into quilt covers and pillowcases. Striped material makes joining widths for bigger covers very simple.*

SCREENPRINTING BED LINEN

Plan the whole design on paper before you begin, and keep referring to it as the screenprinting progresses. The quantity of fabric given below is for a child's single quilt cover.

Materials ★ 4½yd/4m striped fabric (47in/120cm minimum width) ★ 39in/100cm striped fabric for each pillowcase (47in/120cm minimum width) ★ Wooden stencil frame stretched with medium-coarse screen mesh ★ 1 wooden-handled squeegee, same width as screen ★ Fabric ink made with binder and dye colors ★ Cartridge paper ★ Exacto knife ★ Masking tape ★ Brown paper ★ Iron and cloth for pressing

1 Cut out a star from a sheet of cartridge paper (see page 118 for templates). Anchor the sheet of paper firmly to the screen mesh with masking tape, making sure that all areas of the mesh are blocked off except for the design to be reproduced on the fabric. Mix enough binder and fabric dye color for the whole project, unless different colors are to be used.

3 Lift the screen off the fabric carefully, and leave the ink to dry before embarking on the next star. To speed up drying time, cover the printed star with paper and iron it.

2 Mark the positions of the stars on the fabric using a pen of similar color to the ink. Place the prepared screen over the position of the first star. Pour a column of ink about 1in/2.5cm wide across the top of the screen. Put the squeegee behind the ink and pull it across the screen at an angle of 45 degrees.

4 When all the stars are printed and dry, cover the fabric with another clean cloth and press with a hot iron to make the color truly fast. Then make a quilt cover and pillowcase.

CROWNED WITH STARS

Children look adorable in hats, and these star caps are so light, soft, and comfortable to wear – with no itchy knitting or tight elastic – that there is more than a sporting chance they will be kept on without complaint. The instructions given are for the purple hat, and this will fit an average size baby's head (up to 2 years) and measures 17¾ in/45cm around the forehead. The larger gold cap will fit most children aged 5-10 and has a circumference of 21¾ in/55cm. Adjust the template measurements to scale accordingly. If the lining is to be in a contrasting color buy half the amount of fabric given in one color and half in another color or even different fabric.

MATERIALS

Pattern paper, pen, and scissors
20in/50cm velvet or shot silk
12in x 32in/30cm x 80cm iron-on
interfacing material
1 self-cover button (1¼in/3cm across)
5½yd/5m gold thread for tassels
Pins and dressmaking scissors
Needle and thread to match silk
Basting thread
Sewing machine

Left *For older children, the hat can be finished by sewing a metallic star to the button using gold thread.*

Cut out a paper pattern from the template on page 119 and, laying it on the bias of the fabric, cut out five pieces for the hat itself and five for the lining. Then cut five 3½ in/9cm equilateral triangles from the iron-on interfacing, as shown on the shaded area of the template diagram. Iron the interfacing onto the wrong side of the lining fabric as indicated on page 119, leaving a seam allowance of ¼ in/5mm.

Using the printed template as a guide for

Above *Since the star points stick up when the hat is being worn, the contrasting lining looks particularly effective.*

construction, pin and baste the main hat sections from A to B and join the five sections of the hat together to form a circular cap. Clip and trim the seams. Repeat the process for the five sections of the lining material. Press all seams open.

Turn both the lining and main hat pieces inside out and match them up, right sides together. Pin and baste the pieces together, matching up the points and seams. Stitch nine of the brim seams together (from B to C on the template on page 119), leaving one seam open. Clip and trim these brim seams, and turn the hat right side out through the open seam.

Roll the edges of the final seam inside and hem together neatly. Cover the button with a circle of velvet or silk and stitch it firmly to the apex of the hat. Press back the star points, along the lines where the interfacing ends, so that the brim points stick up when the hat is worn.

Make five gold thread tassels, each measuring about 1¼in/3cm for the points of the hat. Wrap the gold thread around two or three fingers approximately 30 times, then wrap the thread several times around one end of the loops, thread a needle with the free end and stitch through to secure. Sew a tassel to each hat point using spare gold thread, and then cut through the other, looped end of the tassel.

LUCKY STARS

Stars and glamour go hand
in hand; from the prominent actors
of stage and screen to the glitter
of star-spangled gems.
Little wonder then that stars
feature so often on clothes, hats,
shoes, and jewelry.
Just as the fairy godmother used
her star-tipped wand to
transform Cinderella for the ball,
the ideas in this chapter will
bestow a feeling of celebration and
a magical allure on everyone
who wears them.

FELTED SCARF

Felt is a fabric formed without any weaving, by using the natural tendency of fibers of wool and animal hair to interlace and cling together. It is probably best known today as a basic craft material, available in brightly colored squares and used by schoolchildren because it is so easy to work with and doesn't fray. But felt has a formidable ancestry, being one of the most ancient fabrics produced by man. It is made by pounding, shrinking, and then compressing natural materials in a soap solution to give a hardwearing fabric providing ultimate warmth and strength.

Heavily felted caps dating from the early Bronze Age have been found in Danish burial grounds, and the ancient Chinese made shields, armor and even boats out of felt. Nomads in Turkistan built felt tents which lasted lifetimes and were completely weatherproof, and elaborately decorated horse blankets from the Turkomen of Iran show how beautiful feltwork can be.

There is a more recent tradition of felting in factories in the North of England, where huge machines with thousands of needles are used to bind fibers together to make lagging and other industrial fabrics. On Orkney, one of these giant machines has been adapted by designers to make woolen cloth, scarves, and shawls for top fashion houses all over the world.

Right Cut out felt shapes and decorate them with buttons and bold wool stitches.

This scarf is a modern adaptation of feltwork using commercially made felt and appliqué. The background is a good-quality lambs wool scarf, and the designs are drawn on colored felt using stencils. The designs are cut out with very sharp scissors, turned over so the drawn line doesn't show, and sewn very neatly by machine onto the scarf with contrasting thread. Plain and satin-covered buttons can be used for decorating the designs, and of course the finished scarf must be dry-cleaned, as felt will always shrink in water.

To abstract a regular five-point star, take machine-stitched lines from each point to its opposite angle.

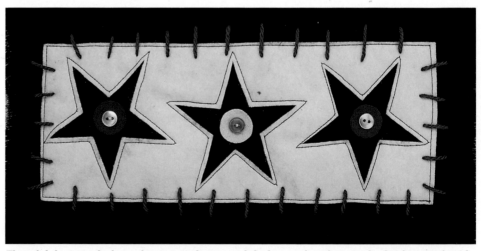

Though laborious, the large darning stitches around the box are best done singly, finishing each with neat knots. Fix a circle of felt in the center of each cut-out star by sewing on a tiny shirt button.

STARS AND SPOTS SWEATER

A sweater created from unbleached yarn dyed with natural plant colors, and knitted in a Fair Isle technique to make it as sturdy and resilient as the strongest cloth, will be treasured as an heirloom and worn by generations. Each hank of this sunset colored yarn is dyed individually, giving shades of red, yellow, and orange along its length, so no two garments knitted from this pattern will ever be the same.

The wool comes from Cheviot sheep in Yorkshire, England. It is dyed by hand and can be ordered direct from the supplier in our directory. It is plied yarn, which means that two strands are mechanically twisted together, making it thicker and quicker to knit up. The pattern is simple, and the Fair Isle technique of weaving the color not being used into the back of the work is easy to pick up. Its square shape makes it uncomplicated, and its generous size looks equally good on men and women.

The naturally creamy yarn is first washed, then fixed with a mordant to allow the yarn to take on and keep a color. For the deep navy, the yarn is then simmered with logwood, and for the sunset colors, two-thirds of each hank is dipped into an onion skin (yellow) bath and left there for 24 hours, then partly dipped into redwood and fustic in turn, to give the oranges and reds in varying degrees.

MATERIALS

24oz/680g navy yarn (A) (see page 127)
16oz/453g mixed red, yellow, and white rainbow yarn (B) (see page 127)
Circular size 3 needle
31½in/80cm long
Set of 4 double-pointed size 3 needles
Pair of size 7 needles
3 circular size 7 needles 16in/40cm, 23½in/ 60cm and 31½in/80cm long
4 stitch holders
Darning needle

MEASUREMENTS

Length from top of shoulder to bottom edge of sweater: 30½in/80cm
Width all around at underarm: 56in/142cm
Sleeve length: 18½in/47cm
Width from cuff to cuff: 57in/145cm

GAUGE

Over pattern, using size 7 needles,
22 stitches and 24 rows to 4in/10cm.

INSTRUCTIONS

Twist yarns at back of work every 1-2 stitches to avoid making holes but do not pull tight.

The sweater is knitted on a circular needle from the top of the flaps to the underarm, so every round of the chart between these 2 points is knit.

When using a circular needle, take great care on the first round to make sure that the stitches are not twisted around the needle.

When knitting in the round, place a short strand of brightly colored yarn between the first and last stitch to mark the beginning of each round, moving it up every few rounds.

The sleeves are knitted on a circular needle from shoulder to cuff, so all rounds are knit unless otherwise stated.

Front flap

* With size 7 needles and A, cast on 150 sts. Join in B and work rows 1-36 inclusive as Chart A. * Slip these sts onto the circular size 7 needle 31½in/80cm long.

Back flap

Work as given for front flap from * to *. Slip these sts onto the circular needle next to sts of front flap (this completes 2 rows of stars). Lay to one side and work pocket linings as follows:

Pocket lining 1

With size 7 needles and A, cast on 34 sts. Beg at st 16 of Chart A, work rows 1-36 inclusive. Slip sts on to a st holder.

Pocket lining 2

With size 7 needles and A, cast on 34 sts.

Right Each star, spot, and moon on this exotic sweater will be different, as the rainbow-colored yarn comes in individually-dyed hanks.

NOTE

*Odd numbered rows are knit worked
from right to left.
Even numbered rows are purl worked
from left to right.*

ABBREVIATIONS

*k: knit; p: purl; st(s): stitch(es);
pat: pattern; st st: stockinette stitch;
rev st st: reverse stockinette stitch;
beg: begin, beginning; cont: continue;
rep: repeat; rem: remaining;
tog: together.*

Below Chart A. **Right** Chart B.

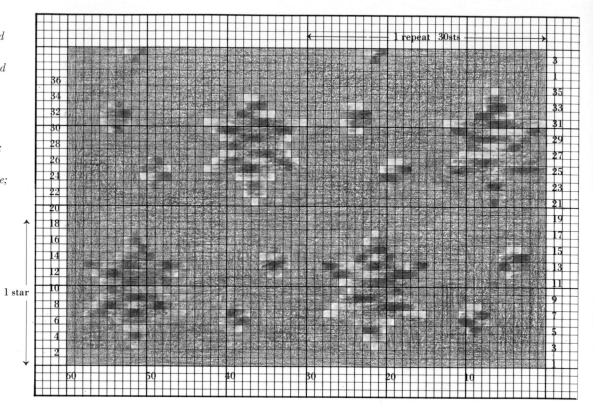

Beg at st 103 of Chart A, work rows 1-36 inclusive. Slip sts on to a st holder.

Return to main body of work and continue as follows:

Round 1 (front, right side facing), pat 15 sts, slip next 34 sts on to a st holder for pocket top 1, pat 34 sts of pocket lining 1, pat 52 sts, slip next 34 sts on to a st holder for pocket top 2, pat 34 sts of pocket lining 2, then pat to end.

Rows 2-36 as Chart B. (This completes 4 rows of stars.)

Rows 37-72 repeat rows 1-36. (This com-pletes 6 rows of stars.)

Rows 73-90 repeat rows 1-18. (This com-pletes 7 rows of stars.)

Divide for front and back

Using size 7 needles and with front and right side facing, work in st st as follows:

Row 91 bind off 14 sts, pat 122 sts, count-ing st already on needle. Turn, leaving rem sts on circular needle.

Row 92 pat 122 sts. Turn.

Rows 93-108 as rows 21-36 of Chart B. (This completes 8 rows of stars.)

Rows 109-122 repeat rows 1-14 of Chart B. Work front neck as follows:

Row 123 (right side facing) pat 45. Turn. Working on these 45 sts, cont as follows:

Row 124 bind off 2 sts, pat to end.

Row 125 as row 17 of Chart B.

Row 126 bind off 2 sts, pat to end. (This completes 9 rows of stars.)

Row 127 as row 19 of chart B.

Row 128 bind off 2 sts, pat to end.

Row 129 as row 21 of Chart B.

Row 130 bind off 2 sts, pat to end.

Row 131 as row 23 of Chart B.

Row 132 bind off 1 st, pat to end.

Row 133 as row 25 of Chart B.

Row 134 bind off 1 st, pat to end (35 sts).

Rows 135-145 as rows 27-36 of Chart B. (This completes 10 rows of stars.) Leave these sts on a spare needle or length of yarn. With right side facing, slip next 32 sts on to a st holder for front neck and cont on rem 45 sts as follows:

Row 123 bind off 2 sts, pat to end.

Row 124 as row 16 of Chart B.

Row 125 bind off 2 sts, pat to end.

Row 126 as row 18 of Chart B. (This com-pletes 9 rows of stars.)

Row 127 bind off 2 sts, pat to end.

Row 128 as row 20 of Chart B.

Row 129 bind off 2 sts, pat to end.

Row 130 as row 22 of Chart B.

Row 131 bind off 1 st, pat to end.

Row 132 as row 24 of Chart B.

Row 133 bind off 1 st, pat to end (35 sts).

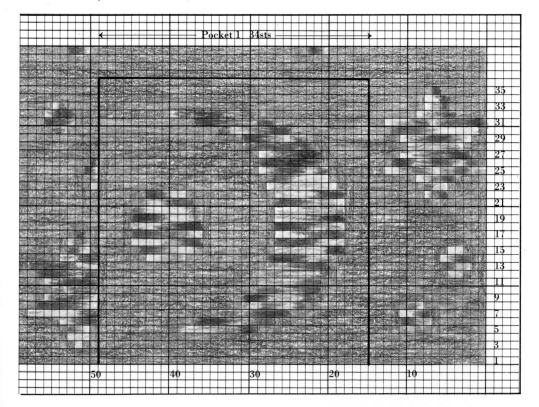

Rows 134-145 as rows 26-36 of Chart B. (This completes 10 rows of stars.) Leave these sts on a spare needle or length of yarn. Return to sts on circular needle for back of garment. Using size 7 needles with right side facing, work in st st and cont as follows:

Row 91 bind off 28 sts, pat 122, counting st already on needle, then bind off 14 sts. Rejoin yarn.

Rows 92-108 as rows 20-36 of Chart B. (This completes 8 rows of stars.)

Rows 109-126 as rows 1-18 of Chart B. (This completes 9 rows of stars)

Rows 127-137 as rows 19-30 of Chart B.

Row 138 (right side facing) pat 39. Turn.

Row 139 bind off 2 sts, pat to end.

Row 140 as row 33 of Chart B.

Row 141 bind off 2 sts, pat to end (35 sts).

Rows 142-143 as rows 35 and 36 of Chart B. Leave these sts on a spare needle or length of yarn.

With right side facing, slip next 44 sts onto holder for back neck and cont on rem 39 sts as follows:

Row 138 bind off 2 sts, pat to end.

Row 139 as row 32 of Chart B.

Left *Truly random hand-dying, in contrast to commercial processes, produces a yarn which appears more painted than dyed. Often, a little of the creamy, natural color will remain giving a soft, variegated effect.*

Row 140 bind off 2 sts, pat to end (35 sts).

Rows 141-143 as rows 34-36 of Chart B. Leave sts on needle.

Slip sts for left front shoulder onto a size 7 needle and, with right sides together, graft left front shoulder to left back shoulder by passing the tip of a third needle through the first st on both holding needles and k tog as 1 st. Repeat for the second st and then lift the first st over the second, and off the right-hand needle to bind off. Continue until all sts have been bound off. Graft right shoulder in same way.

Neckband

With size 3 circular needle and A, with right side facing, k 44 sts for back neck from st holder. Pick up and k 25 sts down left side of neck, k 32 sts for front neck from st holder, then pick up and k 25 sts up right side of neck (126 sts).

Work 8 rounds in k1 p1 ribbing.

Join in B and k 1 round, p 1 round (this is the foldline). Break off B, join in A and work 8 rounds in k1 p1 ribbing. Bind off loosely in ribbing.

Fold band to inside of garment along foldline and slipstitch neatly (and not too tightly) into place using a darning needle and a length of A.

Pocket tops

Slip 34 sts for pocket top 1 from st holder on to a size 3 needle. With right side facing, join in A and k 8 rows. Break off A, join in B, k 1 row, then bind off knitwise.

Work pocket top 2 in same way.

Stitch down pocket linings carefully to wrong side and then stitch sides of pocket tops neatly into place.

Flap edgings

With size 3 circular needle and A, with right side facing, pick up and k 22 sts down right edge of flap, pick up 1 st on corner, then pick up and knit 130 sts along bottom edge, pick up 1 st on corner and then, pick up and k 22 sts up left edge (176 sts).

Beg with a k row, work 4 rows in rev st st. Bind off loosely knitwise.

Rep for other flap.

Where flap edges meet at top of side slits, lay front flap edging over top of back flap edging and stitch together and to body of garment.

Sleeves

With size 7 23½in/60cm long circular needle and A, with right side facing, beg at center of underarm and pick up and k 120 sts along armhole edge. Cont as follows:

Rounds 1-36 as Chart B. (This completes 2 rows of stars.)

Rounds 37-53 as rows 1-17 of Chart B.

Round 54 *k6, k2 tog*. Rep from * to * to end of round (105 sts). (This completes 3 rows of stars.)

Round 55 as row 19 of Chart B.

Round 56 *k5, k2 tog*. Rep from * to * to end of round (90 sts).

Change to 16in/40cm long circular needle.

Rounds 57-72 as rows 21-36 of Chart B. (This completes 4 rows of stars.)

Rounds 73-89 as rows 1-17 of Chart B.

Round 90 *k4, k2 tog*. Rep from * to * to end of round (75 sts). (This completes 5 rows of stars.)

Round 91 as row 19 of Chart B.

Round 92 *k3, k2 tog*. Rep from * to * to end of round (60 sts).

Rounds 93-108 as rows 21-36 of Chart B. (This completes 6 rows of stars.)

Next round change to set of 4 double-pointed size 3 needles and *k2, k2 tog*. Rep from * to * to end of round (45 sts). K 2 rounds.

Next round *k7, k2 tog*. Rep from * to * to end of round (40 sts). Bind off knitwise.

Edging

With set of four size 3 double-pointed needles and A, with right side facing, pick up and k 38 sts along lower edge of sleeve. P 4 rounds, then bind off purlwise.

Finishing

Weave in any loose ends using a darning needle and block the sweater by pinning it to a sheet and coaxing it to the correct length and width measurements. Then cover with a damp cloth and press lightly with a hot iron.

HAT TRICKS

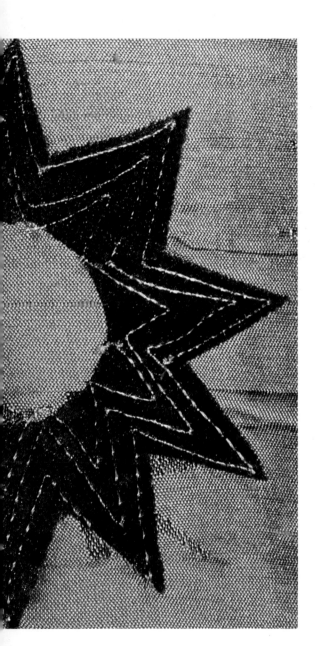

Transform a plain hat with a shimmering hatband. Using star-printed fabric and simple appliqué, the band can be made to fit any hat and can be removed easily. This fabric is silk furnishing fabric, shot with blue and scattered with woven stars.

Measure a length of fabric to fit around your hat, and make it about double the depth of the crown to allow for hemming and pleating. Hem, then fold in three pleats at regular intervals, and don't worry about the folds crossing the pattern of the fabric; in this case they slightly – and intentionally – abstract the blue woven stars. Cut a stencil for the appliqué star: this one has ten irregular points and a hole in the middle. The stars are cut from scarlet panne velvet, which doesn't ravel so won't need hemming. Iron a piece of fusible interfacing to the panne, then trace four stars on the fabric and cut them out. Iron the fused stars onto the background silk.

Thread the sewing machine with embroidery thread on top and metallic thread in the bobbin, so the underneath stitches will glitter through. Then follow the shape of the star with three rows of stitching. Pin the length of appliquéd fabric around the hat and sew in place.

Right *Fix your hat in place with a heavenly hatpin burnished with metallic powder.*

STARS OF THE WILD WEST

Stars appear on the insignia of almost every order of honor and badge of office in the western world, signifying the highest accolade, the greatest achievement.

People who are awarded The Most Noble Order of the Garter, the English order of knighthood founded in 1348, are presented with a garter bearing the order's motto "Honi soit qui mal y pense", and a star medal with the cross of St. George. The Medal of Honor, the foremost military decoration in the United States, is given for "conspicuous gallantry and intrepidity at the risk of life, above and beyond the call of duty" and is suspended from a blue ribbon with a center pad of 13 stars. The army medal is a bronze star; the naval one has a star suspended from an anchor, and the air force design has a star below a thunderbolt.

Perhaps the best known star insignia of all is the sheriff's badge, its six points decorated with little circles and worn with pride on the beefy chests of the keepers-of-the-peace in Wild West movies.

Using craft plastic or Fimo, which is available in gold, silver, and bronze, star-shaped buttons and badges can be made very cheaply and sewn or pinned to jackets, vests, hats, boots, and belts.

The required shapes are cut out of the strips of plastic with a knife and the "firing" is done in an oven, during which the component parts miraculously fuse together. The correct temperature at which to bake the craft plastic is always given on the product's packaging and it varies between different makes, but only takes a few minutes. When it is ready, the high sheen will dull to a convincing metallic glow. As soon as the plastic shapes are taken out of the oven, they will be soft enough to emboss and to pierce with buttonholes before the plastic hardens. When cool, the buttons are ready to wear.

Right *Customize a denim jacket by replacing its buttons with stars made from silver and gold craft plastic.*

Draw and cut out templates for button designs; lay them on the craft plastic and cut round neatly with an exacto knife.

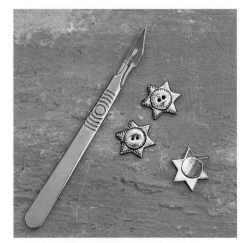

Bake the buttons in the oven, and while the plastic is still warm and soft, make the buttonholes and mark any patterns.

The finished buttons are hardwearing, but will not withstand very high temperatures in the washing machine.

DÉCOUPAGE JEWEL BOX

Use the time-honored art of découpage to make a dramatic jewelry box. Cover a plain wooden box with striking black and white prints, line it with rich satin, and fill it with glittering treasures.

Cutting out pictures and gluing them to objects is as uncomplicated as it sounds, but the skill of découpage comes in finding and assembling the right images for the chosen background and treating them with the correct materials to make them decorative and durable.

Découpage – literally meaning cutting out – is a form of ornamentation that has been used ever since the invention of paper, and it became very popular in the eighteenth and nineteenth centuries, when women of leisure occupied themselves by cutting out specially reproduced lithographs and etchings. The culmination of this was a bestselling book published in 1780 containing 1,500 prints to be cut out and glued, tellingly named *The Ladies' Amusement Book*.

There have, of course, been endless historical examples of beautiful and highly skilled découpage. Serious eighteenth-century découpers intended their work to imitate painting and were very successful. Priceless Chinese lacquerware was copied using papier-mâché furniture covered in gesso and decorated with hand-tinted prints and varnished. Unfortunately, the nature of the materials used has meant that very little of this wonderful "Art Provo" or "japanned" work has survived, but it was tremendously sought after at the time. In the eighteenth century, découpage was used much more simply: whole rooms were painted cream or yellow, pasted with black and white prints, and called print rooms.

Today there is another wide revival in the art of découpage, greatly helped by the technology of the photocopier. Successful découpage relies on strong, thin paper, and often employs images taken out of their original context and repeated several times. Black and white photocopies can be hand-tinted and painted to blend in with the background color of the object being decorated, or can become an integral part of trompe l'oeil wall decoration. Also there is such a proliferation of well-designed visual material on paper nowadays – magazines, newspapers, wrapping paper, cards, shopping bags, and posters – that the bank of available images for découpage is very rich.

Images look much more effective if they are themed. Try to find drawings in a particular style and of a single subject, or use reproductions of similar painted objects by one or two artists. On the box opposite the images are reproduced from the works of two seventeenth-century philosophers who used diagrams to try to explain their wildly extravagant theories. Covering an entire surface will take up more images than at first thought, so roughly cut and assemble them first. The essential process is to get the composition right. Always lay the images out dry in their positions before begining to glue.

Almost any surface can be découpaged: cardboard, wood, glass, metal, leather, walls, doors, and furniture, but the important thing is to prepare it properly first. Varnished or waxed items need washing with mineral spirits; wood needs sanding and any holes need filling; old metal must have the rust removed; new metal should be rinsed with a mixture of vinegar and water and painted with rust-resistant paint; glass and ceramics must be grease, and dust-free; porous backgrounds like leather must be given a clean, even surface, best done by painting with latex paint or ready-prepared acrylic gesso.

Prints and photocopies need sealing and strengthening with a coat of shellac or spray-paint fixative on both sides before gluing. This is often easier to do before

Right *The images used for this box are copied from the drawings of two seventeenth-century philosophers, Robert Fludd and Athanasius Kircher, who interpreted religion and astronomy through cataclysmic heavenly events.*

cutting out. Cut images roughly to begin with, then change to fine scissors or an exacto knife for intricate detail, as accuracy at this point is vital to a professional finish. Use diluted latex paints, acrylic, gouache, artists' watercolors, or artists' oil paints for coloring any images, then craft glue for sticking them down.

Once the image is applied, cover with a soft cloth and run a roller over the print to eliminate any air bubbles. If the surface to be covered has corners, like this jewel box, take special care that they are cut and covered neatly.

Varnishing is essential to découpage, and often up to 20 coats are applied, depending on the finish required. Varnish can give various finishes: it can be clear, tinted, flat, shiny, antiqued, or crackle, but in every case each coat must be allowed to dry and then lightly sanded before the next one is applied. The final polish can be done with wax when the varnish is completely dry all over. Apply a thick coat, leave it for a few hours, polish off, and repeat two or three times with thinner coats of wax for a deep shine.

Left To line an empty box lavishly, use much more satin than seems necessary; turn under and tack the edges with tiny flat-headed tacks, and secure well into the corners.

MIRROR STARS

Mirrored glass catches the light like no other medium, imitating the human conception of stars perfectly, glinting and twinkling in the darkness. Used for jewelry by the Greeks, Indians, and Aztecs, mirror is a bolder, more affordable diamond; one that is available to everyone.

The crucial thing to bear in mind when looking for glass to make jewelry from is its thickness. Glass needs to be as thin as possible, in order that the finished piece is light enough to wear. Most of the thinnest mirrored glass, such as that used for make-up mirrors, is the traditional silver color. However, there are domestic mirror tiles available in limited shades of pink, peach, gold, and gray, which can be used very successfully for jewelry making.

Ordinary colored glass can be silvered, but it will change its hue, so the best way to check that you will get the color you want is to take a mirror to the glazier and hold it under the sheet of colored glass to see the final effect.

Tools for the task are minimal. The most valuable element is time: it only takes minutes for resin to set, but hours to cut and assemble the pieces into the right shape and to build up the strength of the piece with resin. These pieces of jewelry are made so that the holding and backing resin hardly shows.

MATERIALS
Mirrored glass and glasscutter
Pliers
Tinfoil
Polyester resin (a mask should be worn when working with resin for long periods)
Modeling clay
Fine wire
Brooch or earring backings
Exacto knife and toothbrush

Score the glass into triangular pieces and strips with a glasscutter, then reduce them to mosaic pieces with pliers. Lay the pieces out close together and face up on tinfoil until you are satisfied with the design.

Above and right *Sharp-pointed stars look wonderful in mirror jewelry.*

Tinfoil is the best material to peel away from resin.

Once the jigsaw is complete, mix the resin and dribble it all around the edge of the design. It will seep underneath the brooch or earring to hold the pieces together firmly enough for the next stage. Leave to set for between three and five minutes, depending on the manufacturer's instructions. Then peel off the tinfoil.

Put a piece of modeling clay on the front of the piece and turn it face down on the tinfoil to work on the back. Coat the edges and the back of the piece with several layers of resin, leaving each one to dry for 10 to 15 minutes. Incorporate some very fine wire between two or three of the resin layers, primarily for strength, but the wire can also be used to hang any dangling pieces from.

Embed the brooch or earring backing into the final layer of resin. Use a craft knife and water to remove any excess resin from the front and edges of the piece. To finish, polish with a toothbrush.

There are several alternative techniques. For instance, the resin can be mixed first and the pieces of glass pushed into it. This conventional mosaic technique leaves more of the resin showing around the edge and between the mirror fragments, rather like grouting. This can be painted with a couple of coats of enamel or gold paint.

STAR FEASTS

Set your table for a magical
celebration.
Keep the decoration simple,
using clean, fresh colors for cloths
and napkins, tall gold-rimmed
glasses, and star-sprinkled china.
Avoid the temptation to
overload the table with ornaments,
but bring in bold colors
with the food: bright fruits in a
dramatic bowl, pies filled
with jewel-like berries, and a rich
three-chocolate cake.
As the lights go down, fill the
center of the table with
twinkling candles.

★ 45 ★

FROSTED STARS

This delicate tablecloth and two matching napkins will contribute towards making the perfect setting for a romantic, intimate dinner. The translucent cloth with its simple appliquéd stars and fine embroidery will look beautiful in candlelight, and the design is subtle enough to look effective against any china and glass.

Cotton organdy has a light, airy, crisp, and sparky character which is ideal for interpreting a frosty night sky full of stars and crescent moons. Though its transparency poses design questions for seams and thread ends, organdy is otherwise very easy to work with.

The tablecloth is circular (39in/100cm in diameter), and the napkins semicircular (24in/60cm in diameter). Both are stitched entirely by machine and are made from a single width of organdy so that no seams are necessary (see Figure 1). The tablecloth has a double chevron edge finished with close zigzag stitches in two shades of blue. It is decorated in the center with stars and moons stitched in four different shades of blue, plus gray, green, and pale yellow. The moons are stitched two or three times, each time using a different color. The texture of the stitching is varied by using a mixture of silk and cotton threads of different thicknesses and by changing the size of the stitches on the machine.

Stars are either appliquéd or stitched. The appliquéd stars are made from two triangles laid one over the other to form a star shape, and further decorated with intersecting lines of overstitching. The stitched stars are either six-pointed made from two triangles, or five-pointed, sewn in one continuous line, starting at the top of a point and changing direction at each of the other points. Moons are sewn with a mixture of straight and zigzag stitches.

One of the great advantages of using organdy to make this tablecloth is that it washes so well. Even after continual pressing, steaming, and dampening during making, no water marks are left behind. Because of the embroidery, it is best to handwash the cloth in a gentle detergent and press it from the wrong side while not quite dry, using steam or a damp cloth.

Alternative fabrics can be used, but will give a slightly different effect. Voile has the same translucent quality, but is much softer and more loosely woven. As the edge of this cloth is finished with zigzag stitch only (i.e. the edges are not turned in), the fabric must be fairly tightly woven if it is not to ravel, so care must be taken that the particular voile used is suitable. Lightweight linen lawns or cotton lawns could also be used, given the proviso above, but the transparent effect would be lost.

MAKING THE TABLECLOTH

MATERIALS
Large sheet of pattern paper
Paper-cutting scissors
Ruler and protractor
Pins
3yd/2.6m organdy (43in/110cm wide)
Steam iron
Tapemeasure
Soft lead pencil
Dressmaking scissors
Thread: 1 spool each of 4 different blue threads ranging from ice-blue to turquoise; 1spool of pale green; 3 spools of light gray; 1 spool of dark gray
(a darker shade than all the other colors);
1 spool of light yellow
Sewing machine with zigzag stitch and embroidery foot
Small, sharp embroidery scissors
Embroidery hoop

DRAWING THE PAPER PATTERN
Draw a circle 39in/100cm in diameter on the paper, and cut out. Fold the circle accurately into four. Mark a line 3in/7.5cm inside the circumference. Using a protractor, divide the outer cut edge into 10 pencil points. Divide the inner circumference line into 9 points, spaced equidistantly between

Left *Crisp, frosty stars are sewn with a combination of machine embroidery and appliqué.*

the outer edge points (see Figure 2). Using a ruler, join these points to form a chevron edge (see Figure 3). Pin the four layers of paper together, pinning into each point, and cut out very carefully. Open out and iron very thoroughly.

CUTTING OUT THE FABRIC

Iron the fabric using plenty of steam, and lay out on a table. Slide the paper pattern under the fabric, lining up the crease lines of the pattern with the grain of the fabric. Allow the fabric to overlap the pattern by ¾in/2cm and hold down with weights.

Using a fairly soft pencil, trace on the fabric over the lines of the chevron points all around the edge. This will be your guideline for sewing on, so you must be able to see it when the fabric is on the machine, but it must be pale enough not to show through the zigzag stitches. Experiment with this on a scrap of fabric.

Remove the paper pattern and cut out the fabric about ¾in/2cm outside the pencil points in a circle. Do not cut into the points. You will end up with a circle with the chevron stitching line marked just inside it. For the second circle, lay the first circle back on the cloth, turning it so that the straight grain (parallel to the selvage) lies at 45 degrees to that below. This helps stop the points from curling up on the finished cloth. Pin the two layers together at each chevron, and carefully cut out the second circle to match the first, again cutting no chevron shapes (see Figure 4).

FINISHING

Decide which two colors to use for the two rows of close zigzag stitches outlining the outer edges of the cloth. Thread the machine with one of these and use the light gray thread on the bobbin (throughout the work). Set to a small close zigzag stitch and use the embroidery foot. Experiment with the stitch size on doubled scraps of organdy trimming back close to the stitches with small, very sharp embroidery scissors until you create an edge which will not ravel but which also does not feel thick and stiff. Note the settings on your machine.

Stitch all around the outer edge on the pencil line. Trim the fabric back hard against the stitches. Now change to the second color, and stitch the inner line using the width of the embroidery foot as a spacer and guide, to give a gap of about ⅝ in/ 15mm. If you prefer, draw a straight pencil line inside and parallel to the stitched line, as a guide for the inner line of stitching.

Right *The generous napkins look equally elegant when rolled and simply tied to give a flourish of crisp points.*

Turn to the wrong side and cut away one layer of fabric from inside the second row of stitching, so that the area between the two rows remains double, forming a hem all around the edge (see Figure 5).

Keep the cutaway central area for one of the napkins.

DECORATING THE CENTER

The stars and moons can be of varying sizes and placed haphazardly, or all the same size and positioned to make a regular pattern. Using leftover pieces of organdy, cut the triangles for the appliquéd stars slightly larger than the required finished size. Pin each star, complete, in place until you are happy with the position and shape. Then remove the top triangle and, using the embroidery hoop, sew on the lower triangle with zigzag stitch and trim the spare fabric away. Lay on the second triangle, appliqué that in place using a different color thread and trim again. Decorate with lines of straight stitches in different colors (see Figure 6). The size of the zigzag stitches can either be constant, or can be varied along each side of the triangles. Start with a fairly close zigzag at the point, and alter the stitch length and zigzag width button to make a larger, more open zigzag. Turn the buttons as you stitch to achieve a gradual increase, and then slowly decrease to finish at the

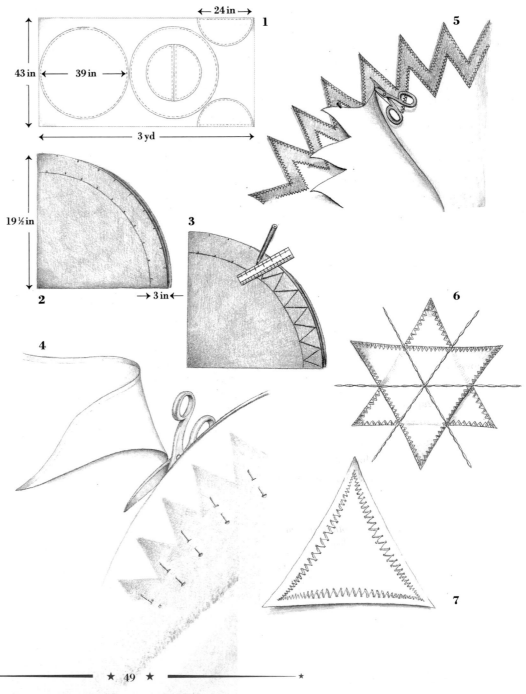

point with a similar size stitch to the one you started with. This takes a little practice, so experiment on scraps first (see Figure 7).

Draw the stitched stars and moons on paper first and trace on the fabric with a soft pencil as before. Stitch around each shape three times with various colors and finish the thread ends neatly. Do this by starting halfway down one side of each triangle, stitching around the rest and finishing over the beginning with a few backstitches. For the moons, vary where you make the seams so that some start at the middle and some at the points, as the line looks slightly heavier where the seam comes. Work the stars in groups, depending on the size of your embroidery hoop. Work toward the edge of the cloth and make them more sparse as you move outward. Press each group of stars on the wrong side to keep the cloth flat. Fill in any large gaps with tiny stars sewn in one row of stitching.

The napkins are made in exactly the same way as the tablecloth, but using semi-circles and with a machine-hemmed straight edge.

Right *A small, translucent cloth with deep chevron edges looks prettiest when laid over a full-length colored cloth, but a larger one could easily be made by joining widths of organdy and making the seams part of the overall design.*

STAR ICEBOWL

The most atmospheric lighting for a celebration table is undoubtedly natural flames. Instead of using candlesticks, float wide, short candles in bowls of water, or better still in a star-shaped icebowl. Sprinkled through with iridescent stars, it will shine and twinkle in the light, and avoid the risk of falling candlesticks and hot dripping wax.

An icebowl can be made in advance, wrapped in plastic freezer wrap and stored in the freezer until you need it. Use distilled water for a really transparent, glinting effect – tap water will result in a much more opaque bowl.

Put a 3-4in/8-10cm deep star-shaped cake pan on a firm, flat tray and half-fill with cold distilled water. Mix several handfuls of iridescent plastic stars in the water. Different sizes and weights of stars are effective so that some will float and others will sink.

Making sure that the freezer shelf is completely horizontal and secure, leave the bowl to freeze for 1-2 hours, until the water around the edges is beginning to ice up.

Remove from the freezer and put a lightweight small round bowl inside the cake pan, positioning corks or crumpled tinfoil around it to center it, and floating it on the water, using weights to settle the bowl at the right level. Return the cake pan to the freezer until the surface of the water has iced over and the bowl is securely fixed.

Remove the pan from the freezer and pour in more distilled water to just below the rim of the small bowl. Sprinkle more iridescent stars in the water, taking care not to allow the water to overflow into the bowl. Return the pan to the freezer until the water has completely frozen all the way through.

Carefully fill the small central bowl with hot water to melt the ice just enough to help you remove it. Then turn the cake pan upside down and pour hot water over it to release the icebowl. Wrap it in freezerwrap and store it in the freezer.

When the table is laid and the food is ready, take out the icebowl and put it on a cloth napkin on a wide glass or silver plate which will reflect the ice and the flames. Fill the central well with cold water and float the candles on it. The icebowl will take hours to melt, but just keep an eye on the plate in case it overflows with water.

As a variation, the icebowl could have flowers or fruit frozen into it at the same stages as the iridescent stars, or the water might be dyed with food coloring before it is poured into the mold.

Right *A star icebowl in the center of the table is like a temporary sculpture: over several hours it will gradually disappear.*

PAPERWORK

Bright, light, and versatile: papier-mâché objects made by talented craftspeople today have a very contemporary image. Using no rare, specialized, or expensive materials – just waste paper, glue, and paint – and involving no artificial light or heat in the process, papier mâché is a craft that is easily approachable, fun, and environmentally sound. Yet it is almost as old as papermaking itself, with known examples from the ancient Near East and China, beautifully decorated with Oriental motifs and handsomely lacquered. Its French name (literally meaning chewed paper) dates from the seventeenth century.

Picture framing was probably the original use of papier mâché in seventeenth- and eighteenth-century England, but it was soon pioneered by makers of trays, firescreens, sewing chairs, and sofas, who pressure-molded sheets of glue-soaked paper into panels. Smaller decorative objects were molded by hand and often inlaid with mother-of-pearl. But widespread popularity did not arrive until the late eighteenth century, when an English craftsman, Henry Clay, developed a version he called Claysware. Horace Walpole's furnishings at his Gothic house in Strawberry Hill near London included a writing desk in Claysware, and from then on, Birmingham became the center of a flourishing

Victorian papier mâché industry. Today the craft enjoys worldwide art form status.

Different processes have been used through the ages, but the basic ingredients remain the same. Paper and glue are mixed together, either to a pulp or using soaked strips of torn paper, and are molded around a framework of balloons, ordinary household objects, shaped wire, or clay. There have been times when sand and chalk have been added to pulped paper and glue, and the resulting mixture has been baked and polished to give a brittle, hard, and shiny surface. But the most popular technique is the laminating method, whereby small strips of paper are built up in even layers, using white glue for strength.

Papier mâché has traditionally been a craft for furniture and ornament, but with the development of suitably strong non-toxic varnishes, it is increasingly used for tableware. Many contemporary papier mâché artists use bright colors, strong designs, and bold shapes which are perfect for trays, napkin rings, and for bowls and platters to hold fruit and bread.

Left *The slightly mottled, distressed blue background on these bowls is achieved by painting with white latex and covering with thin layers of gouache and crayon, then varnishing with a flat, non-toxic varnish.*

PAPIER-MÂCHÉ FRUIT BOWL

A fruit bowl needs to be capacious to hold everything from summer berries to autumn fruits. This bowl is molded on a metal lampshade, which gives a wide, elegant shape, then varnished thoroughly with a good non-toxic varnish.

Materials ★ *1 large newspaper* ★ *Several sheets of waste plain paper* ★ *Flat-bottomed metal lampshade or plastic or china bowl for mold* ★ *Petroleum jelly* ★ *White glue* ★ *Masking tape* ★ *Sharp exacto knife* ★ *Scissors* ★ *Thin cardboard* ★ *Flat white latex paint* ★ *Paintbrush* ★ *Pencil and eraser* ★ *Colored gouache paints* ★ *Clear non-toxic watercolor varnish*

1 Tear newspaper and plain paper into strips 4-6in/10-15cm long and ¾-1½in/2-4cm wide. Smear a thin layer of petroleum jelly over the mold. Mix the glue with a little water and start pasting the paper onto the mold, a layer at a time. Use newspaper for one layer, then plain paper for the next, to ensure a consistent thickness. Apply 8-10 layers, leaving each to dry before applying the next.

3 Paint the bowl with two coats of white latex paint to give a good surface for your design. Leave to dry completely.

2 Trim the top and bottom edges of the bowl with scissors. Insert a knife gently between the mold and the papier-mâché shell, and separate the two. Bind the top edge of the bowl carefully with more strips of glued paper. Cut a circle of cardboard to fit the base and secure it with masking tape to the outside. Remove the bowl from the mold, then cover both the inside and outside with two layers of glued strips.

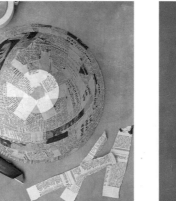

4 Using a soft pencil and eraser, lightly draw your design on the painted surface. Fill in the design with gouache paints and leave to dry. When thoroughly dry, varnish the bowl with two layers of clear varnish.

JUST DESSERTS

Make a star cake for the grandest celebration: put ground almonds in the mixture for richness, and use white chocolate instead of icing.

CHOCOLATE STAR CAKE
Serves 12

1½ sticks sweet butter, softened
⅔ cup sugar
⅔ cup dark chocolate chips, melted
1½ tablespoons dark rum
6 eggs, separated
½ cup and 2 tablespoons self-rising flour
¼ cup ground almonds
Glaze
3 tablespoons apricot preserves
1 teaspoon lemon juice
Decorations and coating
⅛ cup dark chocolate chips
⅛ cup milk chocolate chips
1 pound white chocolate

Preheat the oven to 325°. Grease and carefully line the base of a 12in/30cm star-shaped cake pan.

Cream the butter and sugar together until soft and pale, then beat in the chocolate, rum, and egg yolks.

Combine the flour and ground almonds, then fold into the chocolate mixture. Beat the egg whites until stiff and carefully fold them in until evenly combined.

Transfer the mix to the prepared pan, spreading it well into the points of the star. Bake for 1¼ hours until risen and firm to the touch and a skewer inserted into the center comes out clean. Cool for 10 minutes, then turn out onto a wire rack, and leave to cool completely.

To make the glaze, melt the preserves with the lemon juice and 2 teaspoons water in a small pan. Bring to a boil, then simmer for 1 minute, stirring. Remove from the heat and brush over the top and sides of the cooled cake. Leave to set for 2 hours.

To make the decorations, glue a sheet of white paper to a piece of cardboard. Using a

Above *Make sure the piped chocolate stars are firmly set before lifting the edges with a palette knife and peeling off the parchment paper.*

Right *Keep the cake refrigerated until it is ready to serve, keeping the chocolate crisp.*

2in/5cm star-shaped cutter as a guide, draw seven stars in a line on the paper. Repeat this twice more, each time using a slightly smaller star cutter. Secure a sheet of parchment paper over the top of the white paper.

Melt the dark chocolate chips in a double boiler over simmering water. Transfer the melted chocolate to an icing bag fitted with a plain No. 2 nozzle. Pipe around the seven largest stars and one of each smaller star to form outlines.

Melt the milk chocolate in the same way and pipe around the six remaining middle-sized stars. Melt ⅛ cup of the white chocolate and pipe outlines of the six remaining small stars. Leave to set.

Melt ¼ cup of the remaining white chocolate and transfer to the icing bag. Fill in one star of each size, coaxing the chocolate with a toothpick.

To decorate the cake, melt the remaining white chocolate. Place the cake on the wire rack over a large cookie sheet. Pour over the melted chocolate all at once, using a knife to smooth the sides.

Leave the coating until almost set, then transfer the cake to a large serving plate. Carefully peel the star decorations off the parchment paper and arrange on the cake.

STAR FRUIT BASKET
Serves 8
2 tablespoons sweet butter, melted
8 sheets of filo pastry, cut into 8in/20cm squares
1½ pounds prepared fresh fruit, such as star
fruit, peaches, strawberries, figs, apricots,
grapes, and cherries, peeled, pitted, and sliced
Whipped cream, to serve

Preheat the oven to 350°. Invert a clean 8in/20cm cake pan over an upside-down mixing bowl and brush the bottom of the pan with the butter.

Place one sheet of pastry over the base of the pan to cover it completely. Brush with butter and place the second sheet over the top, leaving one point to hang at least 2in/5cm over the side. Brush with butter.

Turn the pan slightly and repeat with a third sheet of pastry, to form the next point of the star. Continue with four more sheets to form six overhanging points. Finish by arranging the final sheet to cover the base.

Transfer the pastry-covered pan, still inverted over the bowl, to the oven, and bake for 15 minutes. Remove from the oven and carefully lift out the inner pan to leave the pastry shell intact. Return to the oven on a cookie sheet for 5 minutes until golden. Cool on a wire rack.

Arrange the fruit in the pastry case and serve with whipped cream.

A mixing bowl below the pan allows the filo sheets to hang freely and form the points of the pastry basket.

Brush each sheet of filo pastry generously with melted sweet butter before covering it with the next sheet.

JEWELED TARTS
Makes 6
1 pound puff pastry, defrosted
flour for dusting
milk to glaze
1 cup mixed summer berries, hulled and halved
as necessary
3 tablespoons strawberry jam
1 teaspoon lemon juice
heavy cream, to serve
Crème patissière
1½ tablespoons all-purpose flour
1 tablespoon cornstarch, sifted
⅛ cup superfine sugar
1 egg yolk
2-3 teaspoons orange-flavored juice or liqueur
½ cup milk
½ teaspoon vanilla extract
1 teaspoon finely grated orange rind
3 tablespoons heavy cream

Thinly roll out half the pastry on a lightly floured surface. Using a 5in/12.5cm star-shaped cutter, stamp out six stars, re-rolling the pastry as necessary.

Roll out the remaining pastry and cut out six more stars. Using a 3in/7.5cm star-shaped cutter, stamp out the centers from half the stars.

Previous page *A crisp six-pointed Star Fruit Basket and Jeweled Tarts.*

Brush the edges of the whole stars with a little water and press the hollow star shapes over the top to form patty shells. Transfer to a large cookie sheet and chill the stars for at least 30 minutes.

Meanwhile, preheat the oven to 425°. Brush the edges of the pastry with a little milk to glaze, then bake for 12-15 minutes until risen and golden. Transfer to a wire rack and leave to cool completely.

To make the crème patissière, beat the flour, cornstarch, sugar, egg yolk and juice together to form a smooth paste. Bring the milk to just under boiling point, then whisk it into the paste.

Strain the mixture into a clean pan and cook gently, stirring constantly, for 2 minutes until thickened. Stir in the vanilla extract and orange rind, cover the surface with a sheet of plastic wrap to prevent a skin from forming and leave to cool.

Beat the cream into the crème patissière. Divide between the pastry cases, spreading evenly. Arrange the berries on top.

Melt the jam, lemon juice, and 1 teaspoon of water in a small pan, then boil for 1 minute. Strain to remove seeds and brush over the fruits. Serve with heavy cream within an hour of assembling.

Left *Individual puff pastry tarts full of summer fruits and decorated with mint.*

STARGAZING

Decorating with stars goes
back as far as decorating itself.
From the time when
cave dwellers inscribed rock faces
with stylized natural forms in
earth colors, stars have appeared in
every type of adornment
through history.
They have had particularly
strong romantic, chivalrous, and
medieval associations,
since they were studded into
vaulted castle ceilings and gilded
onto battle banners.
In recent and contemporary
decoration, they have never been
redundant: while checks and
floral designs come and go, stars
remain timeless.

GILDED WALL STENCIL

Sometimes even the most modest wallpaper is too much for a decorative scheme. Instead, take part of a room – above the dado line or a single wall – and adorn it with well-spaced stencils and the simplest gilding techniques.

Materials ★ *Stencil card or cardboard coated with shellac* ★ *Exacto knife* ★ *Pencil and ruler* ★ *Small carpenter's level* ★ *Tapemeasure* ★ *Spray paint (red oxide or yellow ocher)* ★ *Clean cloth* ★ *Talcum powder* ★ *Water-based goldsize* ★ *Small tube of water-based gouache, contrast with the red oxide or yellow ocher base color* ★ *Paintbrush* ★ *1 sheet of Dutch metal leaf for each star* ★ *Absorbent cotton* ★ *Hairspray*

1 Draw a star shape, using the template on page 120, on stencil card and cut out carefully with an exacto knife. Make sure the top and bottom points lie parallel to the edge of the stencil card. With a small carpenter's level placed against the card, position the stencil on the wall and mark a few points through it with a pencil. Use a tapemeasure to work out the positions of all the stars in

3 Mix a little water-based goldsize with a touch of gouache paint to color it, so you can see the area you cover. Rub talcum powder over your hands, and brush a thin layer of the colored goldsize over the sprayed star shape. Follow the instructions on the goldsize label for drying times, but it should take about 10 minutes to achieve the correct tackiness.

2 Mask the area surrounding the position of the first star with newspaper, and holding the stencil firmly over the pencil guidemarks, spray a very light coat of paint through the design. Remove the stencil carefully and, when the paint is dry, rub the whole area including the star with a cloth dipped in talcum powder. This eliminates grease, which makes the metal leaf stick where it should not.

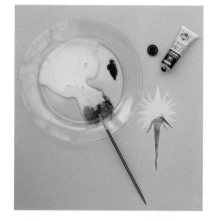

4 Take a sheet of Dutch metal leaf (which is made from brass) and gently press the whole sheet evenly against the tacky surface. After 30 minutes gently polish off the excess leaf from around the design with a large piece of absorbent cotton to reveal perfect edges. Protect the brass from tarnishing with a light spray of hairspray.

PLASTER STARS

Decorative plaster moldings – cornices, corbels, ceiling roses – have been an integral part of period interiors since the eighteenth century. Before that, all interior architectural ornamentation was carved or modeled. Generally, the grander the house, the more plaster work there was, although it was not necessarily more ornate. Victorian plasterwork, even in simple row houses, tended to reach the heights of convoluted decoration compared with the cleaner designs of Georgian and Regency work. Plaster moldings can now be bought in a variety of period styles, but for small items it can be more satisfying to experiment at home using casting plaster and your own simple molds.

The main proviso to making plaster in this way is that the object from which the cast is made must not be undercut in its carving so as to leave pieces overhanging the base. This is why stars are a perfect shape – it is easy to carve a star, unlike a flower or a face, without undercutting the clay at any point.

Plaster casts are very delicate, and larger architectural pieces are always reinforced with fiber. The body of small casts can be strengthened with scrim or wire, but the finer points will always be vulnerable. The plaster takes a couple of days to dry completely, and can then be hung on the wall.

MATERIALS

Modeling clay and tools
Marble tile or board with plastic stretched
tightly over it
Cake pan with removable bottom
Adhesive tape
Silicone rubber and catalyst
(enough for a thin mold over your model)
Casting plaster
Scrim or wire
Shellac and paint
Varnish and finishing wax

Above *After a coat of shellac, any paint can be used to paint plaster casts.*

Using a marble tile or plastic-covered board to make a completely flat base, carve a simple star out of clay, taking care that no shapes are undercut.

Remove the bottom from the cake pan and place the pan over the clay model. In this way, a cast can be taken before the clay is dry to avoid cracks appearing. Seal the pan to the tile or board with tape.

Mix the silicone rubber with the catalyst and pour a small amount over the clay to form a thin mold. Leave overnight. Mix plaster with water to the consistency on the product instructions and pour over the rubber and clay to a depth at least 1in/2.5cm greater than the highest point of the model. This makes a really solid mold.

When dry, remove the pan and separate the clay model, rubber mold, and plaster mold. Replace the rubber mold in the plaster mold and fill with fresh plaster. Bury a little scrim or wire well into the wet plaster to strengthen it. Make sure the surface is flat and lay a loop of wire for hanging in the plaster just before it sets hard.

When completely dry, carefully separate the molds and cast, then apply a coat of shellac to seal the plaster before painting, varnishing, and waxing.

Right *These simple star shapes are especially pleasing because of their alternate straight and wavy points.*

MOSAIC TILES

These vibrant star wall tiles are made from pieces of broken household china.

MATERIALS
Plain white tile
Indelible pen marker
Broken china
Tile nippers
Tile adhesive
Palette knife
Tiling grout and grout color
Toothbrush

MAKING A TILE
Draw the design on the tile and clip the china in pieces of varying shapes.

Working from the center of the tile, put a small amount of cement on one piece of china at a time and glue it down, making sure the sharp edges do not stand too proud. Use rectangular pieces for the border to outline the design. Leave the tile to dry overnight before grouting.

Mix grout with water and dye to the consistency of thick cake mix. Smudge it on by hand wearing rubber gloves and pushing the grout down between each piece of mosaic. Leave for 10 minutes, then take a dry toothbrush and gently brush away the excess from the surface of the mosaic. Leave to rest for a few more minutes, then polish gently with the toothbrush.

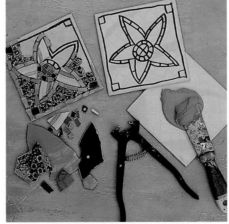

It is a good idea to lay out the pieces to organize the colors and shapes of your design before starting to glue them down.

When brushing, take care not to wear down the grout-filled spaces. After 24 hours the tile can be rubbed clean with water.

RAGS TO RICHES

The exuberance of color and pattern in this rag hearthrug turns on its head the opinion that rag rugs are drab or homely objects born purely out of necessity. The craft of rag-rug making certainly originated from re-using old and worn-out clothes, but is none the poorer for that.

With recycling now at the forefront of consumerism, rag-rug making has taken on greater significance. Yet alongside its economic virtues, it has assumed the mantle of fine art and, increasingly, talented makers are using color like paint and backing fabrics as canvases.

As with any craft, techniques vary, but this rug is made using a hooking method, whereby long strips of old clothing, household rags, upholstery fabric, rubber and plastic bags are hand-hooked through burlap using an oversized crochet hook with a wooden handle.

The hallmarks of this rug and the smaller star wallhangings are their unconventional shapes, their boldness, brightnes, and the density of hooking. More shading than blocking is done on the wallhangings than on the hearthrug, but with both, the star design has a central core from which the colors erupt outward.

Left *Just like a Fair Isle sweater, a multitude of colors is juxtaposed without clashing.*

MAKING THE HEARTHRUG

MATERIALS

39 x 60in/1m x 1.5m drawing paper
Colored pencils or paints
Thick black pen and ruler
Ball of string and thumbtack
Long-blade heavy-duty scissors
39in x 60in/1m x 1.5m burlap
(12 holes per inch)
Thin cardboard or fabric to make template
Large tapestry frame
Rug hook
Assortment of waste materials
Burlap, same size as rug, for backing
White glue and iron

The finished rug measures about 33in/84cm along the straight edge, and is 17½in/45cm deep, but can be made for any size of hearth or doorway. Just make sure there is a generous border of burlap (at least 6in/15cm) outside the design.

A general guide to quantity of rags is that half a pound is enough to cover a square foot, but most rugmakers allow a little extra. Any textures can be used, but the best effect comes with solid or simply striped fabrics and plastics, such as old T-shirts, nylon lining, crimplene, blankets, lurex, and rubber gloves. The width of cut strips depends on the texture. Wool should be cut into ¼in/5mm strips, whereas nylon and

fine silk can be cut into ¾in/2cm strips.

Sketch the design on paper to size (you may need to join several pieces together to make a large sheet), and color it in to act as a guide for hooking materials. To draw a semicircle, make a mark at the center of the straight edge line and cut a piece of string to the length of the radius of the rug. Knot one end of the string and tack the knot to the pen mark with a thumbtack. Attach the other end of the string to the black marker pen, and draw a semicircle as if using a compass. Using the same method but with shorter string, draw another semicircle 2in/5cm inside the first one to make the border line. Trace the main shapes from

Mark the main shapes on the burlap using a template cut from thin cardboard or fabric. Shade in the definite color change areas.

Cut strips of fabric on the straight grain, never on the bias, and begin hooking from the center outward to keep control of the design.

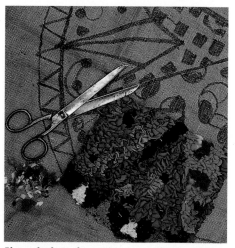

Shear the loops by cutting across them as if you were cutting a miniature lawn. Keep the height level and repeat as necessary.

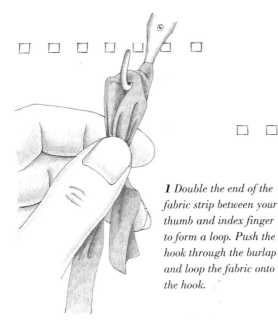

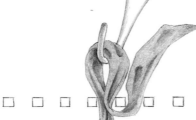

1 *Double the end of the fabric strip between your thumb and index finger to form a loop. Push the hook through the burlap and loop the fabric onto the hook.*

2 *Pull the hook back through the burlap and pull the tail of the strip through to the top side. Make a second loop below the burlap and pull through with the hook to anchor the strip.*

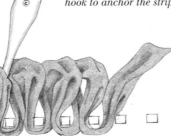

3 *Feeding the strip onto the hook from below, continue pulling loops of fabric through the burlap so that they stand about ¾in/2cm above the surface.*

4 *Continue hooking, forming rows of loop pile, until the desired area is filled. Pull both ends of each strip up above the burlap so the pile cannot come undone.*

your drawing onto cardboard or fabric, and cut out templates. Mark the shapes on the burlap and shade main color areas.

Fix the uncut burlap on a tapestry or similar frame. Always starting from the center, hook through approximately every other hole in the burlap (see diagrams for hooking method). Continue hooking until a small patch has been worked, then shear the loops as evenly as possible to a height of about ½in/1cm.

Continue hooking and shearing until the whole design is covered. Wipe away all the little shearings with a damp cloth and remove the rug from the frame, leaving the surrounding burlap intact.

Lay the rug face down on a table and place the backing material on top. Feeling the outline with the marker pen, draw around the rug. Cut out the shape from the backing material to the same size as the finished rug. Spread glue all over the reverse side of the rug, making sure the surface is well covered. Lay the backing on the glue and press it with a hot iron.

Cut the surplus burlap away from the worked rug, but leave about 6in/15cm all around for turning under. Snip the overlapping burlap at about 2in/5cm intervals. Paint the overlaps with glue, turn under, and press down firmly, slightly overlapping on the curved edge. Allow to dry.

PAINTED CHAIR

This design is based on a medieval "diaper" pattern interspaced with stars from a wallpainting in a church in Normandy, France. The original colors were red ocher, black and white, but here they have been adapted to shades of blue.

Materials ★ *Wooden chair* ★ *White or eggshell acrylic paint* ★ *1in/2.5cm paintbrush* ★ *½in/1cm paintbrush* ★ *Ultramarine acrylic paint* ★ *Stencil card or plain cardboard coated with shellac* ★ *Exacto knife* ★ *Pencil, eraser, and ruler* ★ *Modeling clay* ★ *Yellow ocher acrylic paint* ★ *Small artists' paintbrushes* ★ *Medium and thick gold paint pens* ★ *Water-based clear acrylic varnish*

1 Use a solid old wooden chair with uncomplicated lines. Sand and prepare the chair with two coats of white eggshell or acrylic paint tinted with a little ultramarine. When dry, paint a bright ultramarine blue panel on the seat of the chair, echoing the seat's shape, but leaving a border 1½in/3.5cm all around.

3 Mark the "diaper" pattern on the seat using a pencil and ruler and paint in the yellow ocher circles at the junctions of the lines. Draw around the circle outlines with the medium gold pen, put a dot in the middle, and draw over the "diaper" lines with the same pen and a ruler.

2 Take a strip of stencil card about the same width as the chair rails and legs, and cut a straight row of four equidistant diamonds. Anchor the stencil in place with clay and paint through the diamonds with bright ultramarine acrylic paint. Remove card carefully and wipe it before starting the next leg or rail.

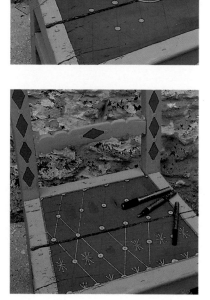

4 With the medium gold pen, draw freehand line stars between the yellow circles. Using a ruler and the same pen, outline the diamonds on the chair rails and legs, and with the thick gold pen and a ruler, draw a line around the blue seat panel. Let all the gold paint dry for 24 hours, then varnish the whole chair.

BLAZING STARS

Stars on quilts have become like butter on bread: a perfect combination and a highly favored choice. From the earliest origins of patchwork quilts, stars have been intrinsic to the craft, appearing in myriad forms far more frequently than any other pattern. Whether the quilt celebrated betrothal, marriage, birth, or a religious, historical, or political event, stars adorned it. In dictionaries, encyclopedias, and pattern books of quilting, hundreds of different star shapes are documented and explained.

As quiltmaking underwent a renaissance in North America among the early settlers, there is natural speculation that celestial navigation on the crossing from the Old World to the New provided inspiration for women as they sewed, but it is perhaps romanticized. The star's endless geometric permutations and its universal connections with celebration probably have much more to do with its preponderance in quilting. From a practical point of view, beautiful star designs can be worked from the smallest scraps of fabric which, in the good old days of creating something from nothing but hard work, was important to the quilters. Many quilts thus contain a variety of differently colored and patterned fabrics.

This quilt is an American example dating from the late nineteenth century, showing a classic Blazing Star pattern worked in a simple red and white color combination. Blazing stars are usually categorized by having eight or more points, and their constituent diamonds are arranged so that concentric rings of color are formed. Despite their age, antique quilts such as this survive in excellent condition and can be seen in many museum collections throughout the country. Traditional patchwork and quilting techniques can be identified and studied in these heirlooms, so historically-inspired quilts can be reproduced very effectively today.

Though it is the most loved quilt design, the star is not the quickest or simplest to work, but can be broken down into basic blocks, in this case of diamonds, triangles, and squares. The work is a long and complex labor of love, but is satisfying and dramatic when completed. The triangular edging, known as prairie points, adds a distinctive character and is found specifically on star quilts. Like countless historical quilts, the block structure makes this one a perfect project to make as a group activity, just as communities of women have been doing for over three centuries.

Right   A quilt is much more than a bedcover; it is the symbol of a family celebration or a life-changing event. Above all, it is a tribute to its maker's skill and an heirloom for the future.

MAKING THE QUILT

The quilt measures 85in x 66¼in/215cm x 167.5cm, excluding the prairie points.

MATERIALS

5yd/4.5m white cotton fabric (36in/92cm wide)
for diamonds, triangles, squares, and borders
2¾yd/2.5m red cotton fabric for diamonds
and prairie points
5yd/4.5m white cotton fabric
(36in/92cm wide) for backing
5yd/4.5m lightweight batting
(36in/92cm wide)
Cardboard and paper for templates
Dressmaking scissors
Pins, needles, and white sewing thread
Iron
Quilting frame
Quilting needles, thread, and thimble
Chinagraph pencil or chalk
Sewing machine

LARGE BLOCK

There are six large blocks in the quilt. Each block is made up of 40 red diamonds, 36 white diamonds, four large triangles, and four large squares (see page 83).

Begin by cutting the diamond patches to form the large star at the center of the block. (Do not cut the triangles and squares until the large star has been completed.) Make a cardboard template by tracing the large

Above *Plan of the quilt.*
Right *Prairie points give a distinctive edge.*

diamond on page 120. Line the template up with the straight grain of the fabric and draw around it with a pencil on the fabric, allowing a ½in/1cm seam allowance all around the diamond. Trace and cut 40 red diamonds and 36 white diamonds.

Use the same template to cut out nine paper diamonds exactly the same size as the template. Place a paper diamond on the wrong side of one of the red fabric diamonds, and pin the paper and fabric together with a single pin at the center. Now fold the seam allowance over the paper and

baste in place all around the edge, sewing through both paper and fabric. Press.

Prepare four more red diamond patches and four white ones in the same way. Holding right sides together, overcast one side of a red patch to one side of a white patch. When piecing diamonds together, always join an edge cut with the grain to an edge cut on the bias. Continue in this way sewing the nine diamond patches together into a larger diamond shape to form one of the eight points of the large block star (see page 83). Make the seven remaining points of the star in the same way, then sew the eight points together to form the large star. Press the star on the wrong side.

The large squares measure 7-7½in/18-19cm when finished. Cut out eight squares each measuring 8¼in x 8¼in/21cm x 21cm from the white fabric. Turn under ½in/1cm along two adjacent edges on all eight squares, baste and press. Now attach each square to the large star. Sew the turned-under edges of the squares into the V-shaped spaces between the points of the large star. Leaving a ½in/1cm seam allowance, trim back every other square to form a triangle, completing the large block (see page 83).

Remove the basting and the paper templates, and press the block. Repeat the whole process to make a further five blocks.

SMALL BLOCK

There are six small blocks in the quilt, and they form the corners of the border strips around the large blocks. Each small block is made up of eight red diamonds, four small triangles, and four small squares.

Begin by cutting the diamond patches. (Do not cut the triangles and squares until the star has been completed.) Make a cardboard template by tracing the small diamond on page 120. Using this template, cut out eight red diamonds, allowing a ½in/1cm seam allowance all around as for the larger diamonds. With the same small diamond template, cut out eight paper diamonds exactly the same size as the template. Prepare the patches in the same way as for the large star. Overcast the patches together to form the small star (see page 83), remembering to join an edge cut with the grain to an edge cut on the bias. Press the star on the wrong side.

The small squares measure approximately 1½in/4cm when finished. Cut eight squares measuring 2½in x 2½in/6cm x 6cm from the white fabric. Turn under ½in/1cm along two adjacent edges on all eight squares and baste in place. Press the turned-under edges. Sew the turned-under edges of the squares into the V shapes between the points of the small star. Leaving a ½in/1cm seam allowance, trim

back every other square to form a triangle, so completing the small block.

Remove the basting and the paper templates and press the block. Repeat the whole process to make a further five blocks.

BORDER STRIPS

There are 13 border strips on the quilt. Each border strip measures approximately 24½in x 5¾in/62cm x 14.5cm when finished. Measure the sides of the large and small blocks to check this measurement for your quilt and adjust if necessary.

Leaving a seam allowance of ½in/1cm all around each strip, cut all 13 strips out of white fabric. Sew the border strips, small blocks, and large blocks together to make up the larger quilt pattern (see page 80). Press the completed front of the quilt.

QUILTING

Piece the batting together so that it is large enough to cover the quilt. Piece the backing fabric together as well. Smooth the backing out, wrong side up. Place the batting on top of the backing, then place the pieced front right side up on top of the padding. Smooth out and pin the three layers together. Lightly mark the pattern on the pieced front with chalk or a chinagraph pencil. The marks can be rubbed off with a cloth when the quilting is complete. Stretch the three

layers on a quilting frame and quilt each section as follows:

The border strips are quilted with cross-hatched lines which are positioned diagonally at a 45 degree angle and are 1in/2.5cm apart.

Each diamond on the large block star is quilted ¼in/6mm from the edge all around the patch. See page 121 for the quilting pattern for the larger squares. The triangles are quilted in the same way as the squares, but using only half of the pattern.

The diamonds of the small star are quilted in the same way as the diamonds of the large star. Each small square is quilted with a horizontal and a vertical line running through the center of the square. The small triangles are stitched all around ¼in/6mm from the edge as for the diamonds.

Using a frame means that the material is less likely to pull as you work. As quilting is a long process, it is useful to be able to leave the work set up to work on at any time. When the quilting is complete, remove the quilt from the frame.

PRAIRIE POINT EDGING

Cut 45 squares from the red fabric, each measuring 4½in x 4½in/11.5cm x 11.5cm. Cut each square in half diagonally to form 90 triangles. Fold each triangle in half and machine stitch along the open shorter side

small square

small triangle

large triangle

large square

one point

large block

large block

small block

border strip

½ in/1cm from the edge. Turn the triangles right side out and press.

Evenly spacing the triangles, pin 25 of them along one long side of the quilt, placing the triangles on the front of the quilt and lining up the raw edges so that the points of the triangles point inward. Pin 25 triangles to the other long side in the same way.

Cut four strips of white fabric 1½ in/4cm wide, two the same length as your quilt and two the same width, piecing these edging strips together if necessary. Pin one of the long strips along one long side of the front of the quilt on top of the pinned triangles, lining up the raw edge with the edge of the quilt. Machine stitch the edging strip and triangles to the quilt ½ in/1cm from the edge. Fold the edging strip over and press to the wrong side so that the triangles turn through 180 degrees and stick out from the side of the quilt. Slipstitch the edging strip in place on the wrong side of the quilt. Sew the pinned triangles and remaining long edging strip to the other long side of the quilt in the same way. Repeat the process for the shorter sides of the quilt, pinning 20 triangles across the top and bottom, and finish as for the longer sides.

Left *The construction of the large block and the small block, the arrangement of border strips, and the quilting patterns.*

SEWING STARS

Needlework was born of necessity: people needed clothes, so animal skins were sewn together with needles of thorn or bone. Ornamentation followed necessity, and there is evidence of creative needlework going back as far as the Byzantine and Egyptian Coptic eras. Two distinct styles of needle and thread work are found in most world cultures: a freestyle embroidery on varying background materials, and a more rigid, counted stitchwork using coarse linen or open-weave fabric, known as tapestry or canvas embroidery.

Today, embroidery has become a leader of originality and pioneering experimentation in the development of the modern craft movement. Though based on a tradition that was interrupted and undermined by mechanization in the nineteenth century, embroidery has adapted and evolved into a mold-breaking branch of art using many different media.

One of the most influential periods of embroidery began in England in the thirteenth century, known as the Opus Anglicanum. Most of the work was ecclesiastical, but it was also in great demand by royalty and nobility because of the gold and silver threadwork, rich colors, and the application of seed pearls and semi-precious stones. Here began the tradition of the professional embroiderer, who served a seven-year apprenticeship before being allowed to work on prized vestments. In the fifteenth century, Flanders took over as the center of western embroidery, but the Tudor period heralded another great era in English needlework, particularly work on canvas, and by the reign of Elizabeth I, domestic embroidery was extremely popular in every social stratum.

Samplers and paneled carpets made communally by women became popular in the seventeenth century. Crewel work – using woolen yarn on cotton and linen – also appeared and was further developed when it was taken to America by the new settlers. The beginning of the eighteenth century saw a marked return to more practical embroidery: there were fewer pictures and wallhangings and an increase in upholstery and screenwork.

The Arts and Crafts Movement, founded in the nineteenth century, was a response to the inferior, mass-produced machinework which came with industrialization. The movement fostered high standards of work and design, and stimulated the development of embroidery into what it is today, a rich tradition of self-expression embracing endless styles and media. Appliqué, hand and machine stitchwork, ribbons, collage, paints and dyes, wood, metal and plastic are just a few of the materials and techniques used by contemporary embroidery and needlework artists.

REACH FOR THE STARS

The machine embroidery shown opposite is an example of a combination of ancient influences, modern techniques, and a fine-art approach. The delicately but densely embroidered textiles of the Opus Anglicanum originally inspired the artist, though this work is done using a sewing machine threaded with fine mercerized cotton and worked on an open-weave linen union background cloth. The image is thoroughly planned on paper before stitching begins, just like a painter might make a pencil or wash sketch to work from. The image is traced through onto the linen and painted, and then the stitching is built up gradually until the surface is completely covered. Though the piece is small, it is a slow and lengthy process, each picture taking several days to complete.

The two singing lovebirds are contained in a deep-based frame of stitches suggesting an open-fronted birdhouse. The mood is one of celebration and wonderment, and the swirling, evenly-sized stitches and gentle angles guide the eye upward.

Right *Dream imagery of stars and lovebirds, densely embroidered by machine.*

MAKING THE PICTURE

MATERIALS
Sketch pad and pencils
Tracing paper and black pen
Open-weave linen union, bleached white
(enough for the picture and for a backing
cloth of the same size)
Embroidery hoop
Water-soluble pen or pencil
Fabric paints to match thread colors
Paintbrush and dishes to mix paint
Iron
Mercerized cottons in chosen colours
Sewing machine
Iron-on fusible fabric

Work out your design on paper in detail, and decide on the size and colors to be used for the finished picture. Trace a good original image onto tracing paper with clean black pen lines.

Fix the bleached linen very tightly in the embroidery hoop, and with the drawing underneath, trace the image through onto the fabric with a water-soluble pen or a pencil. It is important to keep the linen as tight as possible in the embroidery hoop to prevent any puckering as you sew.

Mix the fabric paints until they correspond to your thread colors. Paint accurately on the linen, filling in each area of color and fix by ironing the linen.

Depending on your sewing machine, drop the stitch feeder teeth on the sewing machine, or cover them with the metal plate, as you need to control the direction and length of stitches yourself. Thread the machine with mercerized cotton, and build up the stitches over the painted color blocks until the picture is complete, holding the picture up to the light from time to time to make sure all areas of fabric are covered.

Remove the finished picture from the hoop, trim excess material to ¾in/2cm and fold it back onto the reverse of the picture. Attach the backing cloth using iron-on fusible fabric.

Paint fabric colors on to the drawn design on the stretched linen as a guide for sewing.

Gradually build up the layers of stitching, color by color leaving no linen showing.

Before framing, spray the picture with water to remove traces of the pen drawing.

THE SHOOTING STAR

There are no rules about needlework as fine art, and appliqué is perhaps the most exciting example of the diversity of materials and techniques employed by contemporary artists. The delicate piece, above, is made using several small-scale patterned and solid pieces of fabric, juxtaposed, hand-sewn together, decorated with more stitches, and embellished with metallic stars to make an exquisite self-framed landscape of trees in a night sky.

Its painterly quality is due to the way this artist approaches her work, translating images from her own everyday environment and memories of childhood into visual compositions. The pictures are built up as she goes along, again echoing the way a painter might work, composition being more important than any other element. It is a slow and painstaking process. The result is a development of naive folk art with an uncluttered sampler-like effect.

Pieces of material are chosen from buckets of waste and recycled fabric; they are laid down and picked up, changed for the balance of color, shape, and tone. Usually the base and border start off the process, and often pieces are dyed with vegetable colors to achieve the right shade.

Above *Different stitches add texture and depth to this fine appliqué picture, breaking up plain fabrics and suggesting movement, as in the bright star moving across the sky.*

Each fabric shape is pinned in position before any sewing is done, then the edges are gently rolled under and sewn in place by hand. The quality of hand-sewing is essential to the finished result, the stitches being deliberately exploited to enhance the texture of the woven cloth, and acting like light between brushstrokes of paint. Sometimes an odd bead, button, or sequin is added for a particular effect.

STARLIGHT

This metal lampshade casts a heavenly galaxy of stars on the ceiling and a glow around the room. It is made from a cake pan, which is then distressed by baking it in the oven at a high temperature. Remember that when using a metal bulbholder as a pendant fitting, it is essential that it is earthed.

Materials ★ *Large star-shaped cake pan* ★ *Awl or large sharp nail* ★ *Short ruler* ★ *Hammer* ★ *Heavy-duty screwdriver* ★ *Metal bulbholder complete with shade ring* ★ *Round file* ★ *Steel wool scourer*

1 Using an awl or nail and a ruler, scribe out lines from point to point across the outside base of the cake pan in order to establish a center point. Place the shade ring from the bulbholder on the center and scribe around it.

3 Take a heavy-duty screwdriver and punch more holes inside the circle to break down the little bridges of metal, thereby creating one large hole for the bulbholder. Use a round file to remove any burr or sharp edges.

2 Place the pan on a firm, secure surface, and with a hammer and awl punch a series of holes as close together as possible inside the scribed circle.

4 Using the hammer and awl or nail again, punch a pattern of holes through the base of the pan. Patinate the tin by scrubbing with steel wool and baking in the oven at 450° for 30 minutes. Fit the bulbholder and secure with the shade ring.

CHRISTMAS STARS

Christmas without stars is
unthinkable.
Beginning with the star which
stands above every depiction of the
birthplace of Jesus as a guide
to visitors bearing gifts, to the star
which crowns the Christmas
tree, this image in all its forms
is essential to our traditional visual
celebrations and decorations.
For Christians, the star is closely
tied up with the Christmas story:
the King of Kings, the guiding
light, and the entrance to heaven.
But for everyone, the image is one
to use over and over again to
give a message of jubilation and
goodwill.

STAINED GLASS STARS

Decorating becomes a special pleasure when the box of well-loved Christmas ornaments is brought down from the attic, full of forgotten treasures. These stained glass hanging decorations are sturdy enough to survive many years and will reflect the light in jewel colors.

MATERIALS

Sheet of glass, ³⁄₁₆ in/3mm thick
Glasscutter and pliers
Transparent stained glass paints in red, blue, and green
Black water-based liquid lead for stained glass in a fine-nozzled tube
Paintbrush
Sharp nail or exacto knife
Copper foil tape, ¼ in/5mm wide
Copper wire or jewelry rings
Electric soldering iron
Liquid flux and lead tin solder

Cut the glass using a glasscutter and pliers, or, get it cut at the glaziers. Paint one side of the glass shape with transparent paint, and allow to dry for 10 minutes. Use the fine-nozzled tube of black liquid lead to draw a star design over the transparent paint. Allow to dry for 10 minutes.

Thin some more of the black liquid lead with water in a dish, then turn the glass over and paint the clear side with a thin layer of black. Using a nail or a knife, scratch a similar star shape through the black layer of paint, allowing the design on the other side to show through.

Peel the backing tape off the copper foil and stick it evenly over the cut edges of the glass. Either glue a copper jewelry ring to the top to complete or finish with a soldering iron. Paint liquid flux over the copper foil, then when the iron is hot, apply the solder over it, and solder on a hanging loop of copper wire. Clean the excess flux off with a cloth, and polish well.

Right *Glass decorations can be hung in front of a window to let the light shine through.*

Paint one side with transparent paint, then draw the design over the color in black.

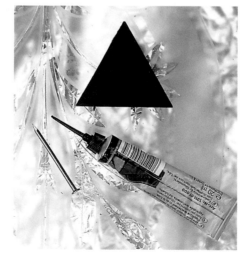

Scrape through the thinned layer of liquid lead on the reverse side to reveal the first design.

Soldering over adhesive copper foil will give a strong silver edge to the glass.

HEAVENLY SWEETS

Though we vary the recipes for the food we eat at Christmas, most of the ingredients have stood the test of time. Spices, nuts, fruit and chocolate, often combined with wines and spirits, have all become part of the tradition of making and giving Christmas sweetmeats.

When made at home with freshly ground almonds, sweet almond paste – or marzipan as it is better known – is something altogether different from its commercial counterpart. Mixed with Christmas flavors and stamped out with star-shaped cutters, it can be used to make a constellation of irresistible candy.

ALMOND PASTE
Makes about 12oz/350g

½ cup powdered sugar
¼ cup superfine sugar
¾ cup ground almonds
½ beaten egg
1 teaspoon lemon juice
a few drops almond extract

Combine the two sugars and almonds in a bowl. Work in the egg, lemon juice, and almond extract to form a smooth paste. Divide into three equal batches. Wrap in plastic wrap and store in the refrigerator until required; the Almond Paste will keep for up to 1 month in the refrigerator.

CHOCOLATE RUMMIES
Makes 8-10

1 batch Almond Paste (see left)
2 teaspoons cocoa powder
1 teaspoon dark rum
1 teaspoon dried instant coffee
⅛ cup ground almonds (optional)
powdered sugar for rolling and cutting

Decoration

¼ cup white chocolate, melted
8-10 chocolate-coated coffee beans

Crumble the Almond Paste into a bowl. Work in the cocoa powder, rum, and dried instant coffee, adding extra ground almonds if the mixture is too sticky.

Wrap in plastic wrap and chill for at least 1 hour. Roll out the paste on a surface lightly dusted with powdered sugar to a rectangle, ½in/1cm thick.

Using a small star-shaped cutter dipped in powdered sugar, cut out 8-10 stars, re-rolling the trimmings as necessary. Cover and chill for at least 4 hours.

Pour a little melted chocolate over the top of each star to coat the top and sides, then place a coffee bean in the center of each. Leave to set on a sheet of baking parchment.

Place in petit-fours cases, if you wish. Store in an airtight container in a cool place for up to 1 week.

GINGER SNAPS
Makes 8-10

1 batch Almond Paste (see left)
½ teaspoon finely chopped stem ginger
½ teaspoon ginger syrup from stem ginger jar
powdered sugar for rolling and cutting

Decoration

powdered sugar
4-5 whole blanched almonds, toasted and halved lengthwise

Crumble the Almond Paste into a bowl. Work in the chopped ginger and syrup until well combined. Wrap in plastic wrap and chill for at least 30 minutes. Roll out the paste on a surface lightly dusted with powdered sugar to a rectangle, ½in/1cm thick.

Using a small star-shaped cutter dipped in powdered sugar, cut out 8-10 stars, re-rolling the trimmings as necessary. Dust lightly with powdered sugar and press half an almond into the center of each star. Cover and store in an airtight container for up to 1 week.

Right Marshmallow Puffs and a selection of marzipan stars – Ginger Snaps, Chocolate Rummies, and Orange and Spice – accompanied by star-shaped glacé fruits The fruits are cut from orange, pineapple and apricot glacé fruits with a small star-shaped cutter and can be dipped in melted chocolate if you wish.

ORANGE AND SPICE

Makes 8-10

1 batch Almond Paste (see page 94)
1 teaspoon finely grated orange rind
½ teaspoon orange-flavored juice or liqueur
½ teaspoon ground mixed spice
1 tablespoon ground almonds (optional)
powdered sugar for rolling and cutting

Decoration

¼ cup dark chocolate, melted
sugared orange slices or crystallized orange
peel, cut into 8-10 small pieces

Crumble the Almond Paste into a bowl. Work in the orange rind, juice, and mixed spice, adding extra ground almonds if the mixture is too sticky. Wrap in plastic wrap and chill for 1 hour. Roll out paste on a surface lightly dusted with powdered sugar to a rectangle, 1cm/½in thick.

Using a small star-shaped cutter dipped in powdered sugar, cut out 8-10 stars, re-rolling the trimmings as necessary. Cover and chill for a further hour.

Pour a little melted chocolate over each star to coat the top and sides. Top each with a piece of orange segment or peel. Leave to set on a sheet of baking parchment.

Place in petit-fours cases, if you wish. Store in an airtight container in a cool place for up to 1 week.

MARSHMALLOW PUFFS

Surprisingly easy to make, these sweet, fluffy stars are always especially popular with children. Marshmallow is simply boiled sugar syrup combined with egg white and gelatin.

Makes 16

1 tablespoon powdered gelatin
1 cup sugar
½ teaspoon liquid glucose
½ teaspoon vanilla extract
1 egg white
pink food coloring (optional)

Coating

⅓ cup powdered sugar
2 tablespoons cornstarch

Grease and line a 7-8in/18-20cm square cake pan with baking parchment.

Sprinkle the gelatin over 3 tablespoons cold water and leave until softened, then stir until dissolved. Heat the sugar and 1¼ cups water in a small pan over a gentle heat, until the sugar is dissolved. Stir in the liquid glucose, increase the heat, and boil the mixture until it reaches the soft ball stage or 240° on a sugar thermometer. Remove from the heat and stir in the gelatin. Transfer to a heatproof bowl and leave until tepid.

Stir in the vanilla extract. Beat the egg white until stiff, then fold into mixture, with a little pink food coloring, if wished. Pour into the pan, tap the bottom to disperse any air bubbles, and chill overnight.

Sift the powdered sugar and cornstarch together and dust half over a sheet of baking parchment. Turn out the marshmallow mixture on top and peel away the lining paper. Using a small star-shaped cutter, cut out 16 stars. Roll the stars in the remaining cornstarch mixture until well coated, then transfer to petit-fours cases or a small plastic container. Serve as soon as possible, as they do not keep for more than a day.

STARS ON A STRING

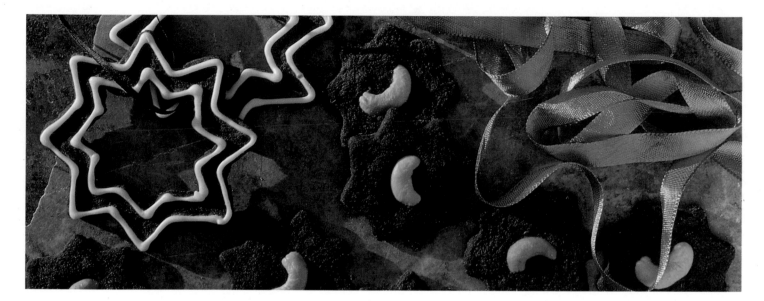

Make a simple buttery cookie mixture and use it as a base to combine with chocolate, spices, and fruity preserves. Hang them as Christmas decorations, but don't expect them to stay there long!

BUTTERY COOKIES

Use either Glacé Icing or melted chocolate to pipe the decorations of your choice on these plain butter cookies.

Makes 12

¼ cup plus 2 tablespoons sweet butter, softened
¼ cup sugar
½ cup all-purpose flour, plus a little extra for rolling and cutting
pinch of salt

Decoration

¼ cup dark chocolate, melted, or a little Glacé Icing (see page 99)

Preheat the oven to 375°. Cream the butter and sugar together, then beat in the flour and salt. Knead quickly on a lightly floured surface. Wrap in plastic wrap and chill for 30 minutes.

Roll out the dough thinly on a lightly floured surface. Using a 3½ in/9cm star-shaped cutter dipped in flour, cut out 12 stars, rerolling the trimmings as necessary. Cut any remaining dough into half-moon shapes with the edge of a circular cutter, if you wish. Transfer to a greased cookie sheet and bake for 15 minutes until crisp and golden. Using a toothpick, make a small hole at the top of each star and leave on the cookie sheet for about 1 minute, then transfer to a wire rack to cool completely.

To decorate, fill an icing bag fitted with a small plain nozzle with melted chocolate or Glacé Icing and pipe different patterns over the stars. Leave to set.

Thread a length of ribbon through each hole, tie the ends together, and use as hanging decorations around the house or on the Christmas tree.

Above *Chocolate Cinnamon Cookies; decorated with nuts or threaded on ribbons.*

CHOCOLATE CINNAMON COOKIES
Makes 12

¼ cup plus 2 tablespoons sweet butter, softened

¼ cup sugar

scant ½ cup all-purpose flour, plus extra for rolling and cutting

2 tablespoons cocoa powder

pinch of salt

¼ teaspoon ground cinnamon

6 cashew nuts, split lengthwise

Decoration

¼ cup white chocolate, melted

Preheat the oven to 375°. Make the cookie dough as for Buttery Cookies (see page 97), using the cocoa powder as a substitute for some of the flour. Wrap in plastic wrap and chill for 30 minutes.

Roll out the dough thinly on a lightly floured surface. Using a 4in/10cm star-shaped cutter dipped in flour, cut out 12 stars. With a smaller star-shaped cutter dipped in flour, cut out the middle from each star. Press a halved cashew nut in each smaller star. Transfer the cookies to a greased cookie sheet and bake for 12-15 minutes, until crisp and golden.

Cool on the sheet for 2 minutes, then transfer to a wire rack to cool completely.

To decorate, drizzle melted chocolate over the outline stars and leave to set.

Tie a piece of ribbon through the middle of each larger star to use as a hanging decoration on the Christmas tree. The smaller solid stars will keep for 2-3 days in an airtight container.

GINGER COOKIES
Makes 8

¼ cup plus 2 tablespoons sweet butter, softened

¼ cup sugar

½ cup all-purpose flour, plus extra for rolling and cutting

pinch of salt

1 teaspoon ground ginger

Decoration

¼ cup chocolate, melted

powdered sugar to dust

Preheat the oven to 375°. Make the dough as for Buttery Cookies (see page 97), mixing in the ground ginger with the other ingredients. Wrap and chill for 30 minutes.

Roll out the dough thinly on a lightly floured surface. Using a 3½in/9cm star-shaped cutter dipped in flour, cut out 8 stars. Re-roll the dough and cut out 8 slightly smaller stars with a different-sized cutter. Transfer to a greased cookie sheet and bake for 10-15 minutes until crisp and golden. Make a small hole at the top of each large star with a toothpick. Cool on the cookie sheet for about 1 minute, then

transfer to a wire rack to cool completely.

To decorate, spread a little melted chocolate over the back of the smaller stars and press one gently onto the center of each large star. Allow to set, thread with ribbon, and hang, if you wish.

JAMMY STAR DODGERS
Makes 6

¼ cup plus 2 tablespoons sweet butter, softened

¼ cup sugar

scant ½ cup all-purpose flour, plus extra for rolling and cutting

pinch of salt

2 tablespoons ground almonds

2 teaspoons finely grated lemon zest

Decoration

½ teaspoon powdered gelatin

4 tablespoons raspberry preserves

1 teaspoon lemon juice

Preheat the oven to 375°. Make the cookie dough as for Buttery Cookies (see page 97), adding the ground almonds and lemon zest with the other ingredients. Wrap in plastic wrap and chill for at least 30 minutes.

Roll out the dough thinly on a lightly floured surface. Using a floured 3½in/9cm star-shaped cutter, cut out 12 stars. With a smaller star-shaped cutter cut out the middle from half the stars. Dampen the edges of the whole stars with a little water, and place

the hollowed-out stars over the top, pressing together gently. Prick the middle of each base star lightly with a fork. Transfer to a cookie sheet and bake for 15 minutes until crisp and golden. Make a small hole at the top of each star and leave on the cookie sheet for about 1 minute, then transfer to a wire rack to cool.

Sprinkle the gelatin over 1 teaspoon cold water, leave until soft, then stir until dissolved. Heat the preserves and lemon juice until melted, then increase the heat and boil for 1 minute. Remove from the heat, stir in the gelatin, then strain. Spoon a little preserves into the middle of each cookie and leave until set. Thread with ribbon and hang, if you wish.

GLACÉ ICING
Makes about ½ cup
1 cup powdered sugar
food colorings

Sift the powdered sugar into a bowl, then, using a wooden spoon, gradually stir in enough boiling water (1-1½ tablespoons) to form a smooth, thick icing with the consistency of heavy cream. Cover the surface with a damp cloth until ready to use.

Left Make big batches of cookies, some to eat fresh, others to decorate the house.

MUSICAL BOXES

In Japan, the ancient tradition of folding paper has reached heights of development unknown through the rest of the world. Complicated ornamental forms are made by folding regular shapes of paper using different combinations of the hundreds of documented folds, without cutting or pasting. The early history of origami is not clear, but it seems to have been a progression from the even older art of folding cloth.

Apart from the Oriental tradition, the folding of colored papers was introduced by Friedrich Froebel into the kindergarten movement he initiated in nineteenth-century Germany. Later, the Bauhaus school of design stressed paperfolding as a method of training students in the theories of commercial design, and it is often used as a test of mathematical skill.

These boxes are made true to the Japanese tradition using squares of paper measuring 8in x 8in/200cm x 200cm (see pages 122-3 for folding instructions). Any paper can be used as long as it is not too thick to fold easily. Here old sheet music from a Christmas carol book has been backed with sheets of silver and gold wrapping paper.

Right *Folded paper boxes make intriguing and suprisingly sturdy wrapping for small Christmas presents and cards.*

ALL WRAPPED UP

Wrapping and opening beautiful parcels at Christmas can be as much a pleasure as the presents themselves. Use rubber stamps or potato cuts in different star shapes to print decorations with gold paint on bright paper. Find tissue paper in white or pretty greens and blues, look out for handmade papers with a more grainy texture, use brown parcel paper, and cut up deckle-edged watercolor paper for cards and tags. Print ribbon by cutting strips of painting canvas and running along it with a star stamp. Using one of the templates from page 125, draw outlines on paper or ribbon and cut them out with a scalpel.

Pack edible gifts in shiny metal boxes with tight lids and tag them with brightly painted tin stars. Add the cookie cutters to homemade cookies, tied on with long bows of gold thread and wrapped with crepe-paper ribbon. Plain star-shaped boxes can be painted different colors and then filled with bright tissue paper printed with stars. Stud the tops of boxes with fake, gaudy beads in jewel colors for precious little presents, and line the boxes with satin or clouds of cotton.

Left and previous page *The tiniest Christmas present lovingly wrapped means so much more than the lavish gift in its shop-bought package, so spend time printing, painting, and writing thoughtful messages.*

STAR BOX

Make a star box to fill with edible presents at Christmas, or make several in various sizes to hide treasures in and to stack on tables as decoration. Using corrugated cardboard sponged with glittering gold and bronze paint, they are deceptively simple and cheap to make.

Materials ★ *Exacto knife* ★ *Paper-covered corrugated cardboard* ★ *Cutting mat* ★ *Scissors* ★ *Gummed brown paper tape* ★ *Masking tape* ★ *Gold and bronze powder paints* ★ *Gum arabic water* ★ *Dishes for mixing paint* ★ *Small paint sponges*

1 Cut out two stars, a base and a lid, from corrugated cardboard (see page 124 for templates). The lid needs to be marginally (¼in/5mm) bigger than the base so that it slightly overlaps the finished box. Cut one strip of cardboard 2in/5cm wide and long enough to bend around the cut edge of the base template. Cut another strip ¾in/2cm wide to act as the restraining lip of the lid.

2 For the base, fold the wider strip along the outside edge of the smaller star, taping it into place using little pieces of masking tape. Using the narrower strip and the bigger star, bend the strip into a star shape about ¾in/2cm inside the edge of the lid, again anchoring it with masking tape.

3 Cut the gummed brown paper tape into 4-6in/10-15cm pieces, moisten each piece as you go, and cover both parts of the box completely, making sure that none of the cardboard is visible. Use small pieces of gummed paper to fill any gaps, and don't worry if the box gets very wet; just leave it somewhere warm for a day to dry out before you paint it.

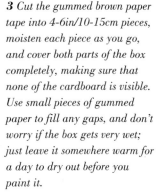

4 With a little gold and bronze powder paint and gum arabic water, mix up a variety of metallic shades in separate dishes. Mix the paint to a fairly thick consistency. Using a different sponge for each color, dab the paint on the inside and outside of both the lid and the base, leaving a deep, lustrous and mottled finish.

CHRISTMAS CARDS

Among the dozens of Christmas cards given and received, the handmade ones stand out from the others and are always best remembered and often kept.

The cards shown here are made from painted silk using a variety of techniques. Once the basic method has been mastered, detailed pieces can be built up on the decorated silk using machine embroidery, layers of wax, and collage. Choose good quality, thick board to mount the silk pictures and cut it to the shape you want. Then either leave it as a plain mat or decorate the card itself: paint it gold, then cover both the inside and outside with tissue paper and use another piece of tissue paper in a different color to frame the silk design.

Any fabric inks can be used for these cards. Special silk paints are available and are necessary if you are decorating clothes or pillow covers, as they can be fixed, enabling the items to be washed safely.

BATIK

Painting on silk is traditionally done using wax as a resist. The wax prevents the inks from running together and achieves a clear outline around the finished image. Special batik tools are available to make it possible to draw on the silk with liquid wax. These have a brass basin to hold the wax and a fine nozzle to apply it to the silk.

The silk needs to be stretched tightly on a wooden frame and anchored with thumbtacks. Batik wax is a blend of paraffin wax and beeswax and needs to be melted using an electric burner. The wax dries quickly while drawing on silk, so the brass basin on the batik tool needs to be constantly refreshed in the melted wax.

Draw the outline of your design directly on the silk with wax or use a stencil. Once the wax is dry, start painting the spaces around the wax using fabric inks.

Above *Machine embroidery and glittering collages held in layers of wax can be built up on top of a painted silk background.*

When the color is dry, unpin the silk from the frame and place it on a piece of brown paper with the wax side uppermost. Put another piece of brown paper on top and carefully iron the sandwiched silk. Repeat the process with clean brown paper until all the wax is removed. Repeat the batik process to build up more color and line.

When all the inks are dry, cut the silk to the size required. Glue it carefully to a separate piece of board and mount it on the tissue-covered card.

OTHER TECHNIQUES

Gutta is another blocking agent which comes in nozzled tubes and in a range of colors, including silver and gold. Unlike wax, it is not removed from the silk after painting is completed.

Stretch the silk in the same way as for batik. Draw your design directly on the silk with the gutta and leave to dry for 15 minutes before starting to paint. When the inks have completely dried, remove the silk from the screen and fix the design by ironing it on the reverse side.

Gold marker pens can be used as a quick and effective alternative to gutta, and no ironing is required to fix them.

Right *Paint larger pieces of silk and cut them up to make cards and gift tags.*

HEAVEN SCENT

Just as the ancient Greeks, Egyptians, and Romans used fragranced flowers, herbs, and exotic spices to invoke the protection of the gods and drive away the evil spirits of illness and death, so the nomadic Hebrew and the Elizabethan mistress of the house believed that where there were strong, good scents, there was less likely to be plague, infection, or pestilence. Natural fragrance has always played a major part in domesticity, and even with our chemicals and sophistication, we still invest time and effort in making our homes, our gardens, and ourselves smell sweet.

In Elizabethan times, fragrant preparations were taken extremely seriously, and the stillroom was a major feature of the house. Flowers and herbs were picked and hung to dry; long wooden shelves held mortars, pestles, spices, and fixatives. Recipes for soaps, candles, disinfectants, cosmetics, and perfumes were passed down from generation to generation, keeping them exclusive to the family. Among their myriad skills, women knew where to find rare scented herbs and grasses; they could get hold of exotic spices and could buy oranges, lemons, and limes. Gradually, women began to have their "stillroom books" published, leaving to posterity their knowledge of perfume and medicine through flowers and herbs.

Of course, we can now buy modern variations of mixtures made by the stillroom mistresses, but the recipes made from flowers grown, dried, or mixed at home are often more subtle and fragrant. These concoctions are known as "potpourri," which literally means "rotten pot," indicating the original moist fermentation of flowers and perfumes. Although we use the same term today, modern methods almost always involve only dried ingredients with drops of scented oil. The recipe here is particularly suitable for making and giving at Christmas. Its deep blues and blacks suggest the midnight sky; the gold pods, star shapes, and seedheads suggest heavenly bodies and planets, and its fragrance is the freshness of Christmas trees mixed with seasonally aromatic spices.

NIGHT SKY POTPOURRI

3 cups blue delphinium flowers, dried
1 cup black mallow flowers, dried
1 cup star tillia
½ cup star anise
½ cup cotton heads
½ cup curly pods, sprayed gold
½ cup liquid amber heads
1 teaspoon spicy pine oil

If you can't find some of these ingredients, either commercially or in your garden,

Right The longer potpourri is left to mature in a closed bag, the longer lasting the scent.

there are many substitutes. Delphiniums can be grown and dried quite easily, but choose the deepest blue variety to dry into the darkest flowers. Black mallow flowers are not actually black when growing, but dry to a deep purplish black. Other flowers which would dry to give a similar effect are the very darkest red peonies and the deepest red roses. Star tillia and star anise are spices which can be found in good Indian and Chinese food stores, and cotton heads could be replaced with batchelor buttons, poppy or marigold seedheads. Dried alium heads could be used instead of liquid amber heads, but be creative: in late summer and fall, don't chop off all the deadheads in your garden; wait for the seedhead, see what it looks like, and it will almost certainly have a decorative use.

MIXING THE POTPOURRI

Combine all the dried ingredients and then drop the spicy pine oil very sparingly onto the flowers and seedheads. Mix it all together very thoroughly and put it in a tightly closed paper bag for at least 2 weeks to mature. Refresh it in 6 months' time with a few more drops of oil and another 2-week spell in a paper bag.

STARSHINE

Christmas is inevitably wintry in the northern hemisphere, so short hours of daylight followed by long nights have made artificial lights an intrinsic part of our decorations. In cities, the bright Christmas lights seem to be twisted around lamps and hung across streets earlier and earlier each year, as if the disappearing evenings herald the onset of celebrations.

Just as candles used to be fixed precariously on Christmas trees long ago, we now string the trees with twinkling mini lights. The prettiest lights are the simplest; small, unshaded incandescent bulbs in plain white, which are the nearest thing to candle flames. Subtle lighting like this will not fight with your other decorations, but will enhance them.

Safety considerations have ended the indulgence of candles on the tree at Christmas, but on a quiet Christmas evening when children are safely in bed, turn off the switches and light dozens of slow-burning beeswax candles, filling the house full of dancing light and the irresistible smell of burning wax.

Left For a different star wreath, twist a string of tiny lights around a wire framework hung with jangling bells, and hang it in the window, where the wire can be pinned around the window frame to the plug, not to leave it hanging.

STAR WREATH

Wreaths are made for remembrance, for celebration, and for simple seasonal tradition. To break from the commonplace circular wreath of twisted holly, ivy, mistletoe, and berries hung on the door at Christmas, make a star-shaped wreath of twigs threaded with golden flowers, seedheads, herbs, and fruit.

MATERIALS
20 straight twigs
Raffia or garden twine
Reel of 0.32mm (30 gauge) florist's wire
0.38mm (28 gauge) stub wires
Florist's scissors
Poppy seedheads, sprayed gold
Dried rosebuds
Dried marigolds
Dried grapefruit slices
Dried bay leaves

The star-shaped framework can be made with single thicker twigs if these are easier to find, as long as they are bound together firmly at all points with raffia or garden twine. Different flower and seedheads can be just as effective, and dried grapefruit slices can be replaced with strips of dried citrus peel. Try to avoid using culinary bay leaves as they are flat and rather crumbly. Instead pick a spray of bay (or another evergreen) and leave to dry hanging in a warm place so the leaves curl up slightly and retain more of their greenness.

CONSTRUCTING THE WREATH
Bind the roses and poppyheads in bunches of three with the stub wires, but use the marigolds singly. Using the florist's wire, start tying the bunches on to the framework as close together as possible to give a dense coverage, and use them in rotation, placing the smaller materials toward the points, so as not to lose the shape of the star. Save the bay leaves till last, and just poke them in between where the color needs breaking up. Finish by attaching a strong wire hanging loop at the back.

Bind together three or four twigs for each side of the star, then tie the five bundles together with raffia at all the joints.

Cut short all stems, then wire the roses and poppyheads together in groups of three before tying them to the wreath.

Bay leaves need no wiring. Stick them firmly in between the flowers and fruit to break up the rich colors.

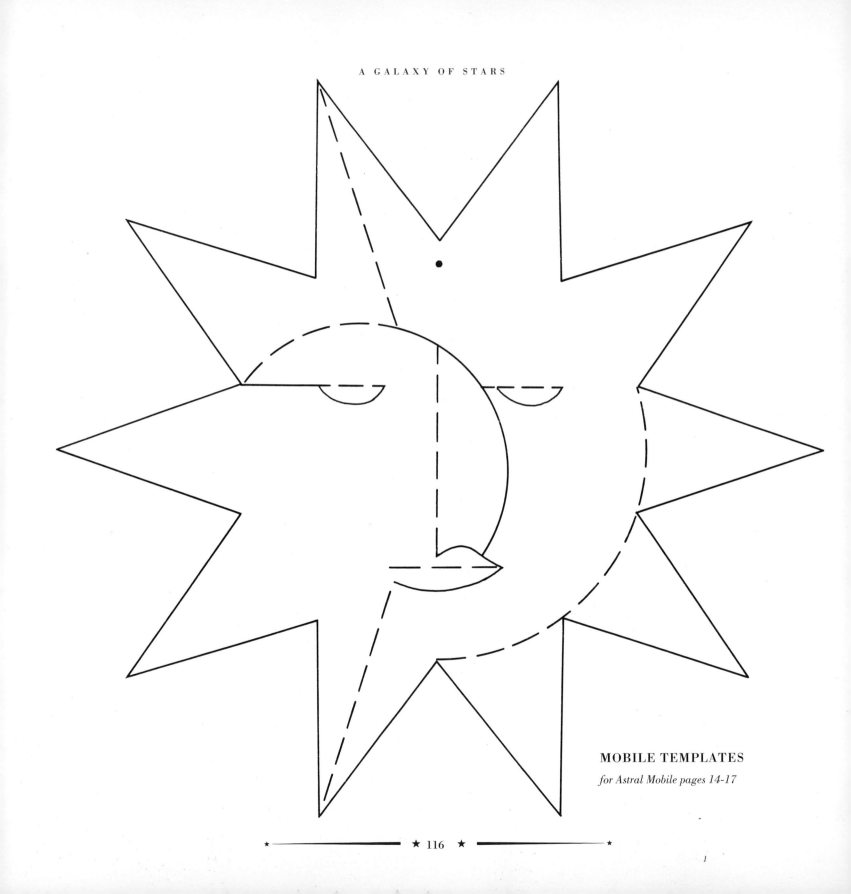

MOBILE TEMPLATES

for Astral Mobile pages 14-17

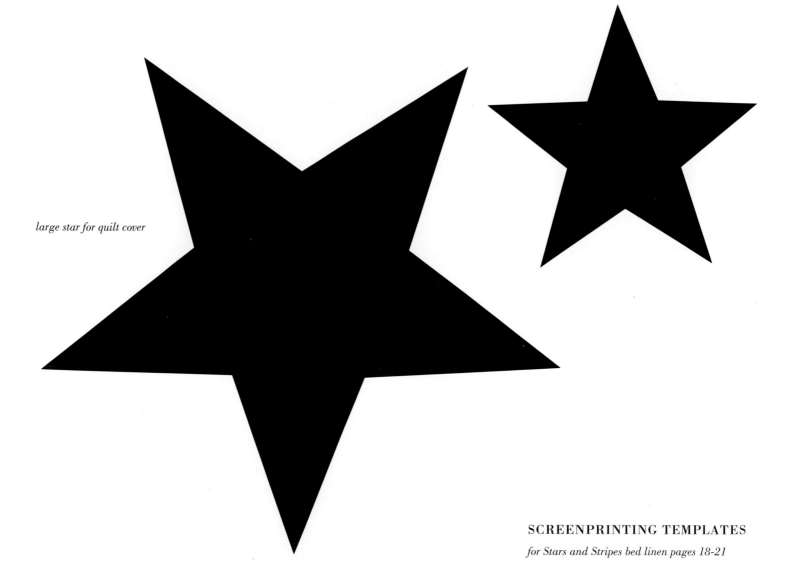

small star for pillowcase

large star for quilt cover

SCREENPRINTING TEMPLATES

for Stars and Stripes bed linen pages 18-21

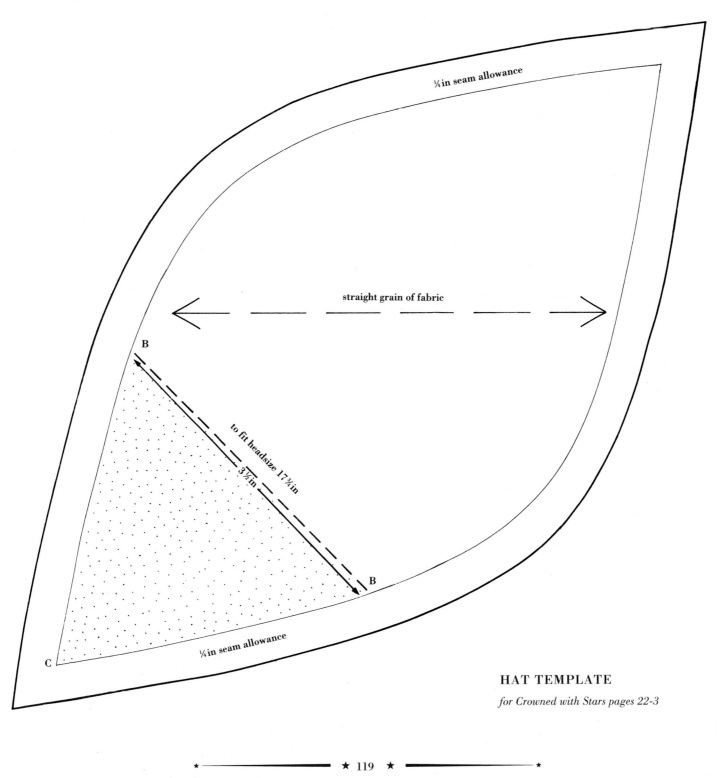

¼ in seam allowance

straight grain of fabric

B

to fit headsize 17¾ in

3½ in

B

¼ in seam allowance

C

HAT TEMPLATE

for Crowned with Stars pages 22-3

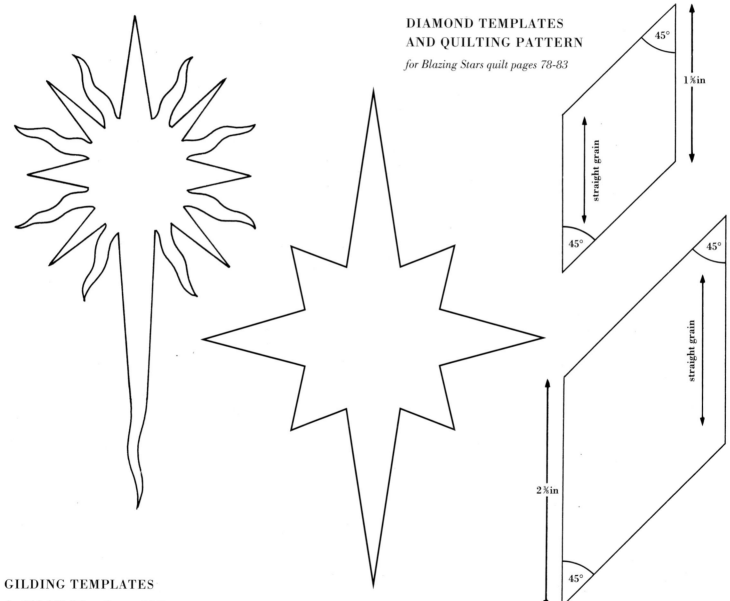

**DIAMOND TEMPLATES
AND QUILTING PATTERN**

for Blazing Stars quilt pages 78-83

45°

1⅜in

straight grain

45°

45°

straight grain

2⅜in

45°

GILDING TEMPLATES

for Gilded Wall Stencil pages 66-7

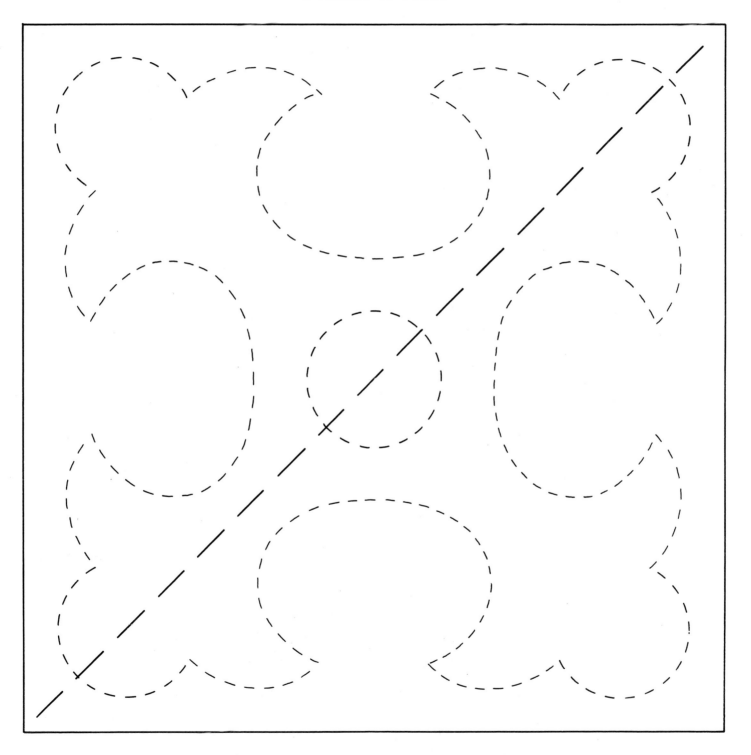

ORIGAMI DIAGRAMS

for Musical Boxes pages 100-101

KEY ——————— VALLEY FOLD ——·—·— MOUNTAIN FOLD

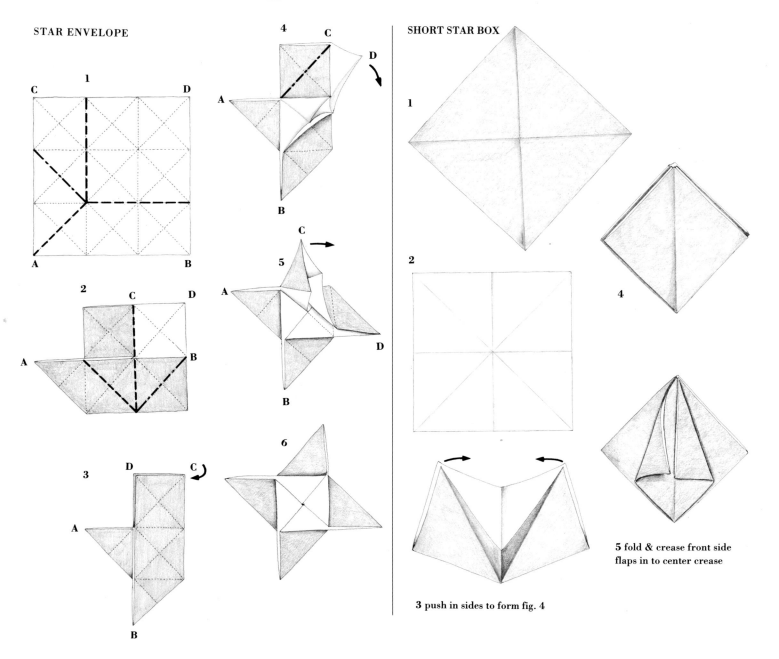

STAR ENVELOPE

1

2

3

4

5

6

SHORT STAR BOX

1

2

3 push in sides to form fig. 4

4

5 fold & crease front side flaps in to center crease

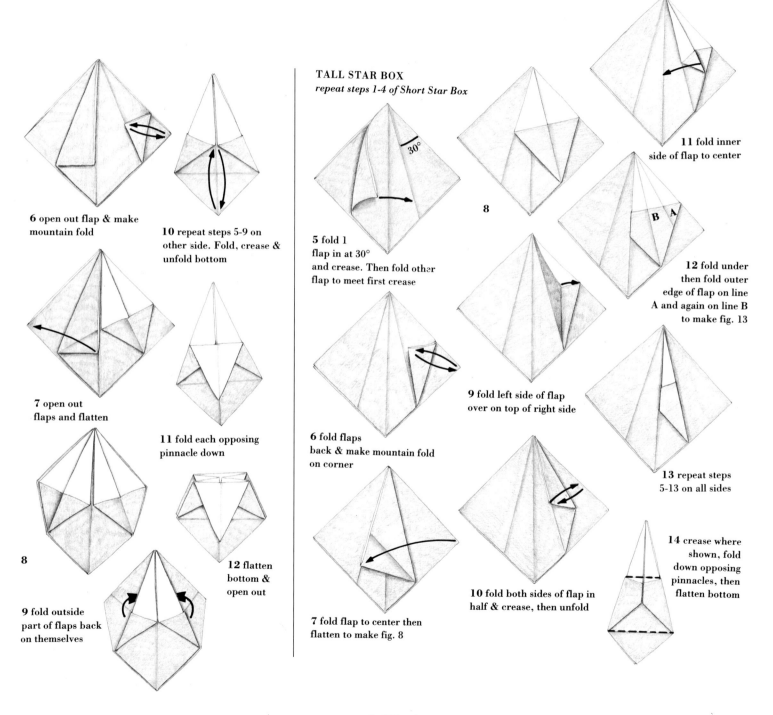

6 open out flap & make mountain fold

10 repeat steps 5-9 on other side. Fold, crease & unfold bottom

7 open out flaps and flatten

11 fold each opposing pinnacle down

8

9 fold outside part of flaps back on themselves

12 flatten bottom & open out

TALL STAR BOX
repeat steps 1-4 of Short Star Box

5 fold 1 flap in at 30° and crease. Then fold other flap to meet first crease

30°

6 fold flaps back & make mountain fold on corner

7 fold flap to center then flatten to make fig. 8

8

9 fold left side of flap over on top of right side

10 fold both sides of flap in half & crease, then unfold

11 fold inner side of flap to center

12 fold under then fold outer edge of flap on line A and again on line B to make fig. 13

B A

13 repeat steps 5-13 on all sides

14 crease where shown, fold down opposing pinnacles, then flatten bottom

STAR TEMPLATES

for Star Box pages 106-7

AN ASSORTMENT OF STARS

CRAFTSPEOPLE AND SUPPLIERS

MADELEINE ADAMS *Papier mâché pp.54-5*
Cobweb Cottage, Stourton Hill, Shipston on
Stour, Warwickshire CV36 5HH
Tel: 0608 84661

FIONA BARNETT *Wreath pp.114-5*
Manic Botanic, 1 Appletree Yard,
London SW1Y 6LD
Tel: 071 930 8128

AILEEN BENNETT *Plastic buttons pp.36-7*
128 Albert Road, London N22 4AH
Tel: 081 888 1649

SARAH BERESFORD
Machine-embroidered hats pp.34-5
199a Upper Street, London N1 1RQ
Tel: 071 704 1641

VICTORIA BLIGHT *Stained glass pp.90-3*
c/o The Black Swan, 2 Bridge Street, Frome,
Somerset BA11 1BB
Tel: 0373 453153

JANET BOLTON *Appliqué picture p.87*
40 Aislibie Road, London SE12 8QQ
Tel: 081 318 3743

VICTORIA BROWN *Star hats pp.22-3*
Bombay Wharf, 59 St Marychurch Street,
London SE16 4JE
Tel: 071 231 2935

SARAH BURNETT *Sweater pp.28-31*
c/o The Natural Dye Company (see Suppliers)

SARAH CROZIER *Hat pins pp.34-5*
47 Exeter Road, Nottingham NG7 6LP
Tel: 0602 622228

MARY FARRELL
Woven wire jewellery pp.24-5, 40-1
Flat 10, 2 Queensdown Road, London E5 8NN
Tel: 081 985 8225

GILL FREER *Plaster stars pp.64-5, 68-9*
35 Windmill Street, London W1

RAY HALSALL
Silk screen pp.18-21, Mirror jewellery pp.42-3
Tel: 071 272 5164
Jewellery available from The Outlaws Club
and Angela Hale *see page 127*

EMMA HICKMOTT
Découpage jewelry box pp.38-41
Unit 18, Portobello Green Arcade,
281 Portobello Road, London W10 5TD
Tel: 081 968 5800

EMMA HOPE *Jeweled shoes pp.24-5*
33 Amwell Street, London EC1R 1UR
Tel: 071 833 2367

JESTER *Fleece slippers p.72*
PO Box 4, Appleby-in-Westmorland,
Cumbria CA16 6BG

MERYL LLOYD *Jeweled boxes pp.102-3*
c/o Conran Octopus, 37 Shelton Street,
London WC2H 9HN

ELEANOR LOVERSEED
Rubber stamps pp.8-13
14 Otago Terrace, Bath, Avon BA1 6SX
Tel: 0225 313161

JANIE MANN *Potpourri pp.110-111*
Charlotte's Garden, Church End House,
Byfield, Northants NN11 6XN
Tel: 0327 61969

KEVIN MCCLOUD
*Gilded wall stencil pp.66-7, Painted chair
pp.76-7, Tin light pp.88-9*
269 Wandsworth Bridge Road,
London SW6 2TX
Tel: 071 371 7151

RACHEL MCDONNELL
Batik and embroidered cards pp.108-9
13 Corporation Oaks, Nottingham NG3 4JY
Tel: 0602 856534

JOHN MITCHELL *Origami boxes pp.100-1*
92 Richmond Road, Kingston-upon-Thames,
Surrey

MUSEUM QUILTS
Blazing star quilt pp.78-83
3rd Floor, 254-258 Goswell Road,
London EC1V 7EB
Tel: 071 490 7732

CLEO MUSSI *Mosaic tiles pp.64-5, 70-1*
The South Bank Craft Centre,
Royal Festival Hall, London SE1 8XX
Tel: 071 928 0681

JENNIE NEAME *Papier-mâché table pp.24-5*
15 Stanley Buildings, Pancras Road,
London NW1 2TD
Tel: 071 278 3045

LOUISE PICKFORD
*Desserts pp.58-63,
Sweets and biscuits pp.94-9, 107*
42 Ferndale Road, London N15 6EE
Tel: 081 802 9420

JANE POULTON
Machine-embroidered picture pp.84-6
c/o Crafts Council, 44a Pentonville Road,
London N1 9BY
Tel: 071 278 7700
Reach For the Stars © Jane Poulton 1993
All rights reserved DACS

LIZZIE REAKES *Rag rugs pp.72-5*
68 Oaklands Road, Hanwell, Ealing,
London W7

GEORGINA RHODES
Decorated papers and tags pp.2, 104-5,
Star box pp.106-7
c/o Conran Octopus, 37 Shelton Street,
London WC2H 9HN

FIONA ROBBINS
Papier-mâché fruit bowl pp.56-7
22 Montpellier Place, Brighton BN1 3BF
Tel: 0273 779 664

FREDDIE ROBINS *Felted scarf pp.26-7*
Unit 5, Cockpit Yard, Northington Street,
London WC1N 2NP
Tel: 071 831 6212
Machine-felted scarves are available from
Tait & Style, Brae Studio, Back Road,
Stromness, Orkney KW16 3AW
Tel: 0856 851186

LOUISE SLATER *Mobile pp.8-9, 14-17*
205 Wandsworth Workshops, 86-96 Garratt
Lane, London SW18 4DJ

SUE THOMPSON
Tablecloth and napkins pp.6, 46-51
c/o Conran Octopus, 37 Shelton Street,
London WC2H 9HN

SUPPLIERS

ART/CRAFT/GRAPHIC
Charrette, 212 East 54th Street
New York, NY 10022

Eaglecrafts, Inc.
168 W. 12th Street, Ogden, UT 84404
(801) 393-3991

Sam Flax
425 Park Avenue, New York, NY 10022
(212) 620-3060

PAINT
Janovic Plaza, 161 Sixth Avenue
New York, NY 10014
(212) 627-1100

Pearl Paint Company, 308 Canal Street
New York, NY 10013
(212) 431-7932

JEWELRY/BEADS/ORNAMENTS
Ornamental Resources, P.O. Box 3013
Idaho Springs, CO 80542
(303) 279-2102

SEWING/KNITTING
Erica Wilson Needle Works, 717 Madison
Avenue, New York, NY 10021
(212) 832-7290

The Natural Dye Company, Stanbridge,
Wimborne, Dorset BH21 4JD, England

Halcyon Yarns, 12 School Street,
Bath ME 04530
(207) 442-7909

The publisher would like to thank the following for their help
with props:
Amadeus, 309a King's Road, London SW3
Angela Hale, 15 Thomas Neal's, Earlham Street, London WC2
Ann May, 80 Wandsworth Bridge Road, London SW6
Atlantic Antiques Centre, 181-183 King's Road, London SW3
Chelsea Gardener, 125 Sydney Street, London SW3
Christopher Gollut, 116 Fulham Road, London SW3
Combined Harvest, 128 Talbot Road, London W11
The Conran Shop, Michelin House, 81 Fulham Road, London SW3
David Wainwright, 251 Portobello Road, London W11
Decorative Living, 271 New King's Road, London SW6
Designers Guild, 271 King's Road, London SW3
The Dining Room Shop, 62-64 White Hart Lane, London SW13
Divertimenti, 139-141 Fulham Road, London SW3
Fergus Cochrane Antiques, 570 King's Road, London SW6
Gallery of Antiques, 2 Church Street, London NW8
Georgina von Etzdorf, 149 Sloane Street, London SW1
Global Village, 247 Fulham Road, London SW3
Graham & Green, 4 Elgin Crescent, London W11
Green & Stone, 259 King's Road, London SW3
Harvey Nichols, 109-125 Knightsbridge, London SW1
Harwood Antiques, 24 Lower Richmond Road, London SW15
Heart & Heart Hatters, 131 St Philip St, London SW8
Hirst Antiques, 59 Pembridge Road, London W11
Jane Churchill, 135 Sloane Street, London SW1
Kips Flowers, 110a Campden Hill Road, London W8
The Knightsbridge Pantry, 12 William Street, London SW1
The Lacquer Chest, 75 Kensington Church Street, London W8
Lindsay Antiques, 99 Kensington Church Street, London W8
Lionheart, 253 Portobello Road, London W11
Magpies, 152 Wandsworth Bridge Road, London SW6
The Outlaws Club, 49 Endell Street, London WC2
Papyrus, 48 Fulham Road, London SW3
Paradise Farm, 132a King's Road, London SW3
Pulbrook & Gould, 127 Sloane Street, London SW1
Rimmington Vian, 5a Iliffe Yard, Crampton Street, London SE17
R. Soles, 109a King's Road, London SW3
V.V. Rouleaux, 201 New King's Road, London SW6
Russell & Bromley, 64-66 King's Road, London SW3
The Shaker Shop, 12 Harcourt Street, London W1
Sweet Pea, New King's Road, London SW6
Themes and Variations, 231 Westbourne Grove, London W11
Tobias & the Angel, 68 White Hart Lane, London SW13
Verandah, 15b Blenheim Crescent, London W8
The Walton Street Stationery Co, 97 Walton Street, London SW3
R. M. Williams Ltd, 15 Kensington Church Street, London W8
O. F. Wilson, Queens Elm Parade, Old Church Street, London SW3
556 (hire), 556 King's Road, London SW6

INDEX

The publisher would like to thank:
Katy Brown for so generously lending her house for location photography;
Susan Jenkins and Museum Quilts for the loan of the Blazing Star quilt,
and Sally Harding for her research and practical help on the project;
Ian Muggeridge for his meticulous work and organisation;
Richard Proctor; Michelle Clark, Beverly Le Blanc, Penny Hill and
Yvonne McAra for their editorial work; Nathalie Hambro for early
inspiration and all the suppliers who have so generously provided
materials and props for the projects.

The author would particularly like to thank:
Jo Mead for her supreme efficiency and encouragement; Georgina Rhodes
for her inspired design; Debbie Patterson for her sumptuous photographs;
Kevin McCloud for his time, talent and invaluable help; Sarah Burnett,
Sue and Eleanor Thompson for their beautiful work; and Rose Patton for
making it all run smoothly.